smokin'

WILLIAM MORROW

An Imprint of HarperCollins*Publishers*

smokin'

Recipes for Smoking Ribs,
Salmon, Chicken, Mozzarella,
and More

with Your

Stovetop Smoker

christopher styler

Designed by William Ruoto

Library of Congress Cataloging-in-Publication Data

Styler, Christopher.
    Smokin' : recipes for smoking ribs, salmon, chicken, mozzarella, and more with your stovetop smoker / Christopher Styler.—1st ed.
        p. cm.
    Includes index.
    ISBN 0-06-054815-0 (pbk.)
    1. Barbecue cookery.   I. Title.

TX840.B3S775   2003
641.76—dc22

                                                                              2003060208

09   10   11   12   13   14   WBC/RRD   10   9   8   7   6   5

To the two Joes in my life

Contents

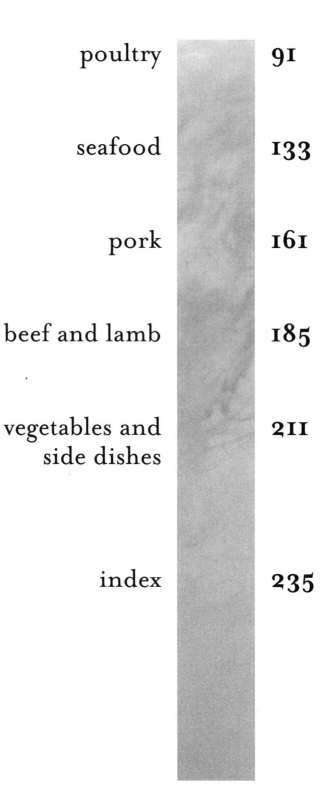

Acknowledgments

Thanks to:

Harriet Bell, for bringing the stovetop smoker and this project to my attention, and for her help and insight while I wrote this book.

Anne and Chris Malone of CM International, who were generous with their products and advice.

Kim Yorio, the best agent and friend a person could hope for.

Joe, for his support and understanding in this project and everything else I undertake.

Introduction

Smoked foods are a lot liked grilled foods. They have a unique depth of flavor that cannot be duplicated using other cooking methods, and, like grilling, there is a simplicity to stovetop smoking that makes it a very approachable way to cook. Even inexperienced cooks can dive right in to smoking their favorite foods on top of the stove.

But preparing smoked foods with a stovetop smoker has advantages over grilling. It requires less of your time: you don't have to hover over the smoker and continually turn or baste foods. Also, smoking is not dependent on the season. No matter what the weather conditions or time of year, your smoker can be a source of juicy, moist foods that are rich in flavor and almost effortless to prepare. You will enjoy using your smoker as much in summer, when the corn is sweetest and the tomatoes and eggplant are ripest as much as you will on a gray winter's day, when a bubbling pot of Split Pea and Smoked Turkey Soup (page 70) fills the bill.

The stovetop smoker's year-round appeal coupled with the ease of its operation are two of the reasons these smokers are finding their way into more and more home kitchens. Not to mention that the food tastes great and can be prepared with virtually no added fat. The recipes that follow will introduce you to the stovetop smoker or, if you're already familiar with home smoking, they'll give you fresh ideas for using it.

Hot smoking foods on your stovetop is as simple as putting together your favorite pasta dish. In this collection of recipes you will find all the information you need for simple to sophisticated dishes. The master recipes at the beginning of the chapters walk you through the process of smoking all kinds of basic ingredients from chicken breasts and beef brisket to shrimp and lamb chops. They also outline smoking times, suggest types of wood to use, and offer seasoning tips and serving suggestions. Some master recipes highlight foods that are enhanced after smoking by a brief spell in a skillet, under a broiler or over a bed of glowing coals. I refer to this process of finishing foods with a second method of cooking as *Combo-Cooking*. Most often, this is optional, but with foods like baby back ribs or skirt steak, it is highly recommended. And with large foods that need a relatively long time to cook, like a whole turkey or brisket, it is mandatory.

It's easy to become a creature of habit. Even after twenty-something years in restaurant and test kitchens, I found myself returning to a few tried-and-true dishes for busy mid-week dinners. With a stovetop smoker, my everyday repertoire has expanded considerably. The more I use my smoker, the more stovetop smoking becomes a part of my daily dinner repertoire. I wrote this book to share my newfound enthusiasm for smoked foods with you. I hope you enjoy it.

What is a stovetop smoker?

An ingenious device that, as its name implies, sits atop your gas or electric stove and captures heat and smoke from smoldering wood chips. The heat and smoke are used to flavor and cook whatever fish, meat, poultry, or vegetables you've chosen. (I'll get more into the anatomy and operation of the smoker in a minute.)

Stovetop smokers are manufactured by Camerons (CM International, Inc.) of Colorado Springs, Colorado (camerons smoker.com). They are available in many cookware specialty shops and even some upscale grocery stores, and come with a get-started guide and a small supply of wood chips. A search of the Internet will reveal scores of online sources, with slight variations in price. But, as always with online shopping, be aware of the cost of shipping.

Stovetop smokers are made of stain-

VERY IMPORTANT!

Before you use a stovetop smoker on a smooth top electric stove, refer to your manufacturer's instruction manual and guide. Many manufacturers advise against placing cookware larger than the burner element over the burner.

less steel that is sturdy enough to stand up to repeated direct contact with heat—both from stove burners and ovens. I used one of my smokers more than a hundred times in four months while testing the recipes in this book. It is no worse for the wear, except for some blackening on the bottom, which is perfectly normal.

A similarly sturdy lid slides onto the body of the smoker. The tight fit between bottom and lid is what holds in heat and smoke during cooking. If you're wondering how to smoke larger items, such as a whole turkey (see Whole Turkey, page 101), wonder no more: When smoking items don't fit under the lid, replace the lid with an aluminum foil tent. Larger items like these are finished in the oven, in which case the foil is simply removed and the smoker doubles as roasting pan.

Camerons manufacturers the smoker in two sizes: the larger measures 15 × 11 × 4 inches deep, sells for around fifty dollars, and holds six boneless chicken breasts comfortably. (You should never crowd too much food into a smoker.) The smaller (around forty dollars) is 11 × 7 × 3 inches deep and holds about three chicken breasts comfortably. I advise purchasing the larger size, even if you're cooking most often for one or two. It is always a good idea to prepare double the amount of what you would normally cook for a meal and use the leftovers in a salad, as a snack, or in a pasta sauce. One of the advantages of cooking foods in a stovetop smoker is that they remain moist and will taste just as good in a day or two as they did right out of the smoker.

How a Stovetop Smoker Works

The stovetop smoker works on a very simple principle. Wood chips are scattered over the bottom of the smoker to produce the smoke that flavors the food inside the smoker. Your stove's burner supplies the heat needed to turn the chips into smoke and heats the inside of the smoker—sort of like a mini-oven—to cook the food. A drip tray, which catches liquid that would otherwise moisten the chips and stop them from smoking, covers the bottom of the smoker. The food is arranged on a wire rack, which sits atop the drip pan. A sturdy sliding lid keeps smoke and heat inside the smoker. With the exception of how to replace the lid with aluminum foil for smoking large items (more on that later) and when to adjust the heat during smoking in a few of these recipes, that's all you need to know. Here is the process laid out in all its simplicity:

- Read through the recipe carefully before you start. Some recipes require seasoning or marinating food in advance; other recipes suggest you brine food or take them to room temperature before smoking.
- Make sure the smoker parts are clean and dry before you start.
- Sprinkle the amount and type of wood chip you have chosen over the center of the bottom of the smoker, covering an area roughly the size of your burner.
- Put the drip pan in place. Always line the drip pan with a single layer of aluminum foil. This cuts cleanup time in half.
- Arrange whatever item(s) you are smoking on the rack. Newer smoker models have nonstick racks; older racks should be sprayed with vegetable cooking spray to prevent sticking and make for easier clean up. Be sure to leave space between items on the rack and between the food and the sides of the smoker.
- Close the lid about two-thirds of the way and center the smoker over a burner. (If what you are smoking will not fit under the cover, see Smoking Large Items, page 5.) Turn the heat to medium.
- When you see the first sign of smoke rising from under the drip pan, close the lid securely and start timing.
- Check the food for doneness at the time suggested in the recipe. Wear oven mitts or protect your hands with sturdy pot holders, grasp the handles firmly with one hand and slide the lid off with the other. Test the food as quickly as possible (with an instant-read thermometer or other methods suggested in the recipe) and slide the lid closed quickly if it needs more cooking time.
- When the food is ready, turn off the heat and remove the lid of the smoker, unless a recipe directs you to leave it on for a specified amount of time.

YOUR SMOKER IS A STEAMER TOO

The tight fit of the smoker lid and bottom make a stovetop smoker an ideal way to lock in steam, just as it locks in smoke and heat. To use your smoker as a steamer, set it up just as you would for smoking (minus the wood chips, of course). Then pour in enough water to come up to within a ½ inch of the smoker rack. Place whatever you're steaming on the rack and bring the water to a gentle boil. Close the lid and start your timing.

That's it. It will probably take you as much time to set up your smoker and start your first batch of smoked foods as it did to read about it. It will take even less time on the next round.

Smoking Large Items

Some foods, such as brisket or turkey, that you will want to smoke don't fit in the smoker with its sliding cover in place. To keep smoke and heat from escaping, you can use aluminum foil. I keep a roll of extra-wide (18-inch) heavy-duty aluminum foil on hand for these occasions, but you can make do with regular 12-inch foil if that's what you have.

First, spray the sides of the smoker with vegetable cooking spray to prevent food from sticking should it come in contact. (Always try to avoid contact, but it will happen occasionally.) After the large item is set on the rack, tear off a piece of 18-inch-wide heavy-duty foil that is longer than the smoker by about 6 inches. Crimp one of the long edges of the foil sheet to the lip along one of the long sides of the smoker. Place your hand over the item on the rack and make sure there is space between the top of it and the foil before crimping the sides of the foil sheet to the sides of the smoker. Now crimp the foil to the shorter sides of the smoker. Lastly, seal the second long edge. Then take a minute to make sure the foil is tightly sealed to the smoker all the way around. Turn on the burner to the medium setting normally used when smoking. Remember, there is no smoker lid to close when you see the first sign of smoke. *The timing in this book for smoking food with aluminum foil in place of the smoker lid starts when you turn on the heat, not when you see the first smoke arise.*

To make a cover using 12-inch-wide aluminum foil, tear off two lengths of aluminum foil, each about 6 inches longer than the smoker. Lay one atop the other and square the edges. Make an even ½-inch fold along one of long edges of both sheets. Make two more ½-inch folds to bind the two sheets together along one edge. Open up the sheets: you will have a large (about 20-inch-wide) sheet of foil made up of the two sheets of foil crimped together along the center. Proceed as above.

Smoking Small or Soft-Textured Items

Don't let small foods like almonds slip through the cracks or, more accurately, through the spaces on the smoking rack. Soft-textured foods like chicken livers (see Smoky Chicken Liver Mousse with Pumpernickel Melba Toasts, page 44) can also be tricky. Place a disposable aluminum foil pan on the smoker rack. Perforate the bottom of the pan liberally (I use a very sturdy meat fork) to allow better circulation of heat and smoke. The size pan that works best is an 8 × 11-inch pan, labeled "broiler pan" in the stores. Lacking that, an 8- or 9-inch square pan works, but offers less space. Individual recipes call for using a foil pan on the smoker rack where appropriate.

Frequently Asked Questions About Stovetop Smoking

HOW DO I GET STARTED?

Start with a simple two-step: Season and smoke. If you like to go trout fishing—and are known to actually catch something—start with a nice cleaned trout. If you hunt down your dinner in the aisles of the local supermarket, start with some boneless chicken breasts. Season the trout or chicken simply with salt and pepper and smoke according to the guidelines on page 138 (trout) or 94 (chicken breasts). While they're smoking, toss together a couple of your favorite side dishes and go from there. Working with familiar foods like these will give you an idea of the flavor that smoking lends to food. The more you smoke, the more you'll know about your own preferences: whether you like a little more smokiness or a little less, for example. Or whether you prefer to rub foods with seasonings before you smoke, or dip or glaze them after they're smoked. Once you get the knack, you can move on to more involved dishes, like the Apple-Cured Pork Tenderloin with Sweet and Sour Cabbage on page 176. You will start to see that smoking isn't an exotic art, it's another fundamental cooking technique like grilling or baking.

WILL MY KITCHEN BE FILLED WITH SMOKE?

Your kitchen should be filled with the aroma of wood smoke mingled with whatever it is you are smoking, but by no means should your kitchen be smoky. If it is, there's something wrong. A tiny amount of smoke sneaking from a corner of the smoker is normal. But any more than a thin stream means your smoker lid needs adjustment. Try this method, suggested in the cooking guide that came with my smoker: Close the smoker lid halfway. Press down lightly on the half of the lid over the smoker with your left hand, then press down firmly on the other half of the lid with your right hand. Press just enough to bend the lid *slightly*. Slide the lid back on; you should feel a little resistance and the lid should now be virtually free of leaks.

HOW DO I KNOW WHICH WOOD TASTES BEST WITH A CERTAIN FOOD?

The same way you get to Carnegie Hall: practice, practice, practice. Although there is not much difference in the flavor of the various wood chips—apple wood doesn't impart an apple flavor, for example—there is a marked difference in the assertiveness of each. I'll divide wood chips loosely and objectively into three camps—milder, medium, and more assertive. Here goes:

> *Mild*: apple, alder, cherry
> *Medium*: oak, maple, bourbon-
>   soaked oak, pecan
> *More assertive*: hickory, mesquite,
>   corncob

There is also what I call the *twang factor*. Certain chips—corncob, pecan, and mesquite come to mind—deliver a distinct twang (for lack of a better word) to finished dishes. I avoid that twang when smoking delicate foods like whitefish fillets and high moisture foods like vegetables.

A SOLDIER IN THE FIGHT TO STAY FIT

You won't have to tell anyone, but hot-smoked foods can be as healthful as they are delicious. You'll notice that the master recipes (those that outline the smoking of pork chops, salmon fillets, or tomatoes, for example) call for adding no fat, except for rubbing certain fish and vegetables lightly with olive oil to prevent their surfaces from drying out during smoking. That makes smoking a fundamentally low-to-no-fat-added way to cook. Also, most foods benefit from a simple rubbing with salt and pepper before smoking, but how much salt you choose is up to you. You'll find that smoking makes a good way to use less salt without missing it.

Lastly—and I repeat this throughout the book—experiment, play, and rely on your own taste buds to end up with the flavor that suits your taste best. My recommendations for the type and amount of wood to use come down on the conservative side. Those of you who like a more gung-ho approach may end up using close to twice my recommended amounts.

WHAT IS MEDIUM HEAT?

Manufacturer's directions call for smoking foods at *medium heat* and, indeed, that's what I use almost all the time. The temperature inside a smoker when it is filled—not over-filled—with food should reach about 350°F in approximately 8 minutes, and stay at or near that temperature throughout the smoking time. But one stove's medium is another stove's low, so how to determine the correct setting for your stovetop smoker? If you have a gas range, it's easy: adjust the flame to halfway between its lowest point and highest point, make a mental note of the gas control dial setting and go from there. Oddly, medium heat is rarely the middle setting on the burner knob. For example, on my range, setting the burner knob to number 7 in a range of 1 to 9 gives me a medium flame.

Here's a foolproof way to determine the right setting on your range: The first time you use your stovetop smoker, determine the medium heat on your range, whether gas or electric, and load the smoker, leaving a little room in the center. Lay an oven thermometer dial side up in the center of the rack and close the lid. Check the temperature after about 5 minutes by sliding the top open and closing it as quickly as possible. Repeat every 4 minutes or so throughout the smoking time to monitor the temperature. Adjust the heat under the smoker as necessary to keep it near 350°F, but don't panic if you're a few degrees off or if the temperature fluctuates a little during smoking. Once you find the setting on your stove knob that gives you a more or less steady 350°F temperature during smoking, you won't have to use the thermometer again.

DO I ALWAYS SMOKE WITH MEDIUM HEAT?

Most of the time, yes, but not always. Sometimes I find it helpful to lower the heat after the wood starts to smoke. Here is the rule of thumb I use: If whatever you are smoking is very large or very small, lower the heat *slightly* after the wood chips start smoking. Lower the heat so small items—like oysters (see Oysters on the Half Shell, page 142)—don't overcook before they take on a smoky flavor. At the other end of the scale, if you're cooking something large, like a turkey (see Whole Turkey, page 101), lower the heat to slow down the amount of smoke the wood gives off. The wood will last longer and have a better chance to penetrate and flavor all that turkey. Directions for lowering the heat slightly are given in the appropriate recipes.

WHAT IS COMBO-COOKING?

Combo-Cooking means combining another method of cooking with smoking to make a better tasting dish. Sometimes it is done to improve the texture of a finished dish—like crisping up the skin on a chicken breast after you've smoked it. Or, combo-cooking is a way to finish cooking something that is too large to be safely and completely cooked in your smoker, like a whole turkey or chicken.

One look at any of the salad recipes in this book shows that I love to combine foods that complement each other in terms of flavor, color, aroma, and with their texture as well. In the case of the Skirt Steak on page 193, I partially cook the steak in the smoker—which can be done up to a day in advance—and finish it on the grill for that crackly outer texture. Similarly, I love crispy-skinned chicken, so when I smoke chicken breasts, I leave the skin on and crisp it up in a nonstick pan after removing the breasts from the smoker. The cleanup takes a minute longer, but the texture and flavor are ten times better. You may prefer your hamburger just as it comes from the smoker—juicy, smoky, and medium rare. I finish my burgers in my trusty cast-iron skillet for a minute on each side to add color, flavor, and texture. You may opt out of any Combo-Cooking that is used to add a finishing texture touch, but when it is used to finish cooking larger items and bring them to a safe-to-eat temperature, it is a necessary step in the smoking process.

A Few Notes on My Experiences with My Stovetop Smoker

• I would never serve a meal of all white foods—poached chicken breast, steamed cauliflower, and mashed potatoes, anyone? Nor would I serve a meal of all smoked foods. Tart, spicy, and slightly sweet flavors bring out and complement the complex, assertive flavor of smoked foods. The honey and mustard that form the dressing base in the Smoked Chicken, Pecan, and Gruyère Salad on page 74 is an example. Similarly, the fresh taste of green vegetables pairs well with smoked meats, poultry, and fish, which is why so many serving suggestions in this book call for simple sides like sautéed spinach or buttered string beans. Serving a garden

A WORD ABOUT SALT

I specify kosher salt in just about every recipe in this book. There are two reasons for this. First, nothing else—like iodine or non-clumping agents—is added to kosher salt, so it tastes cleaner. Second, like most restaurant cooks and chefs, I "grew up" using kosher salt and have adjusted to its coarser grains, which make it easier for me to feel what I'm adding to a dish. If you can't get kosher salt or don't want to be bothered, you can use regular table salt, starting with about two-thirds the recommended amount and adjust from there. The amount of salt used to season items before they are smoked may look like a lot, but keep in mind much of the salt that is rubbed onto food before smoking is lost during the smoking process. Use less if you're on a sodium-restricted diet.

salad dressed with a tart vinaigrette alongside smoked foods is a good way to touch on both these points.

• With experience, you will determine whether you like to rub or marinate foods before you smoke them or if you prefer to give them a quick seasoning with salt and pepper and serve them with a sauce or glaze afterward. Generally speaking, I like salting and peppering before smoking, then dunking or glazing after. Exceptions abound and many recipes throughout the book offer suggestions for rubbing or seasoning foods before they're smoked. Sweet, tart, and spicy flavors complement smoked foods well, while I find herb flavors, whether rubbed on first or added later, work less successfully with smoked foods.

• What's nice about smoking at home instead of relying on store-bought items is the control you have over seasoning and texture. Long before I came into contact with a stovetop smoker, I took to making my split pea soup with smoked turkey wings instead of the more traditional ham hocks. I needed to cook store-bought turkey wings up to an hour before they were tender enough to add the split peas, and if I used enough turkey wings to add a nice portion of meat to each bowl of soup, I found the smoky flavor too strong. When I smoke my own wings for soup, I ease up on the smoke. There is enough turkey meat—and just the right amount of smoky flavor—to go around.

• I rely completely on an instant-read thermometer for testing the doneness of meats and poultry I cook in the smoker. This not only builds in safety to the cooking process but provides a way to check foods quickly for doneness, meaning the smoker lid can be reclosed quickly with minimum heat loss. Appropriate temperatures are given with individual recipes.

• Smoke more than you need for a single meal. Even if you are a two-person household, fill the smoker rack with chicken breasts or cook a brisket for a change. One of the best qualities of hot-smoked foods is their juiciness. Leftover chicken will stay moist in the refrigerator and makes a good addition to salads and pastas. Brisket reheats well, and makes a superb hash or sandwich.

• Once you get the hang of regulating the heat under your smoker, cooking foods so they're all done at the same time should be no problem. You may find, however, that if you're smoking lots of smaller items, like a pound of shrimp, chicken wings, or scallops, that those closer to the center of the rack will cook and color faster than those around the edges. Similarly, you may find that the underside of certain items, like a whole

BASIC BRINE

Determine how much water you will need to cover what you are brining. The best way to do this is to put the item in a container—stockpot, Dutch oven, etc.—that will hold it comfortably. Pour in water, one quart at a time, until the item is completely covered. Lift out the item and stir in 3 tablespoons of sea or kosher salt for every quart of water you added. Set the container of brine on a sturdy refrigerator shelf and slip the item you're brining into it. You may have to remove the shelf above the pot in order to do this. Brine for the specified amount of time. (If lifting a pot full of brine is too difficult, try this: pour off the water after measuring it, place the empty pot on the refrigerator shelf, and refill it with the same amount of water. Add the salt, then return the item you're brining to the pot.)

trout, may color more than the top surface. Because smoking is a slow, even method of cooking, these differences don't really amount to much. But you might check smaller items like the ones mentioned about two-thirds of the way through the suggested smoking time. If pieces around the edge seem to be browning or cooking more slowly than those in the center, remove the smoker lid and rotate items from the edges to the center and vice versa. Replace the lid as quickly as possible to recapture the heat and smoke.

Brining

Brining—soaking foods destined for the smoker in a salt and water solution—carries seasoning all the way to the center of a large item, like a brisket or whole chicken. Sometimes this basic brine is enhanced with sugar or other seasonings. When you roast a turkey in the traditional manner, for example, there is gravy that seasons the meat after carving, but that's not always the case with smoking, so I brine larger items to season them effectively.

Like Combo-Cooking (see page 9), you can opt out of brining, but I suggest trying it once. There is a big flavor pay-off for very little effort.

Safety Pointers and Miscellaneous

• Pot holders: Invest in a pair of heavy-duty pot holders or oven mitts to use when working with your smoker. I buy mine—super-thick terry squares—from a restaurant supply store. They will come in handy when you slide the lid open to check for doneness or when you lift the smoker by its handles to take it off the heat.

• Fire extinguisher: A smoker is no more likely to cause a kitchen fire than any other cooking gear you own. In fact, because there is no splattering grease that can come in contact with an open flame, it is much less likely to start a fire than most other methods of cooking. No kitchen, however, should be without a fully charged fire extinguisher.

• Plan ahead for the end of smoking: You will need a place to set the hot smoker in order to empty it.

• The handles, which fold in alongside the smoker to make it more compact for storage, should always be turned to the side, not extended out in front of the stove, during smoking. And remember to extend the handles before you start smoking. If not, they, like the body of the smoker itself, will get very hot during smoking, which makes them difficult to handle once the smoking has begun. To remove the lid during or after smoking, grasp the handles with a protected hand and slide the lid off with another protected hand.

sauces,
salsas,
and rubs

Smoked Tomato Sauce

There is real depth of flavor to this sauce. It matches beautifully with sautéed or grilled chicken, poached shrimp, hamburgers, or, believe it or not, meatloaf.

MAKES ABOUT 2 CUPS

4 smoked plum tomatoes

3 tablespoons olive oil

3 garlic cloves, thinly sliced

1 small red onion, finely chopped (about ½ cup)

Kosher salt

Pinch red pepper flakes

2 tablespoons chopped fresh cilantro or flat-leaf parsley

1. Smoke the tomatoes according to the directions on page 212. Cool them to room temperature and slip off the skins. Chop them coarsely.

2. Heat the olive oil in a heavy 2-quart saucepan over medium heat. Stir in the garlic and cook, shaking the pan, until you can smell it, about 1 minute. Stir in the onion, season lightly with salt, and add the red pepper flakes. Reduce the heat to medium-low and cook, stirring occasionally, until the onion is softened, about 4 minutes.

3. Stir in the tomatoes and cook until most of their liquid is evaporated, about 5 minutes. Adjust the heat so the sauce is barely simmering. Taste the sauce and add salt to taste if necessary. Cover the pan and cook until the tomatoes are completely tender, about 10 minutes.

4. Pass the tomato sauce through a food mill fitted with the fine disc. If you don't own a food mill, scrape the sauce into a blender and blend, using quick pulses, until the sauce is fairly smooth. Stir in the cilantro. Serve warm. The sauce may be prepared up to three days in advance and stored, covered, in the refrigerator. It may also be frozen for up to two months. Warm the sauce in a small saucepan before serving.

Smoked Tomatillo Sauce

1½ pounds small (about 1½ inches in diameter) fresh tomatillos

1½ tablespoons hickory or mesquite wood chips

2 tablespoons olive oil

2 tablespoons chopped fresh cilantro

2 teaspoons fresh lime juice

1 teaspoon kosher salt, or as needed

Hot red pepper sauce, optional

1. Discard the papery coating from the tomatillos and wash them well. Pat them dry and set them core side down in an 8 × 11-inch perforated aluminum foil pan.

2. Set up the smoker using the wood chips and smoke the tomatillos as described on page 6 until they are browned in spots and softened, about 40 minutes. It is fine if some of the tomatillos split open. Cool to room temperature.

3. Scrape the tomatillos into a food processor or blender. Add the olive oil, cilantro, lime juice, and 1 teaspoon salt. Process until smooth. Check the seasoning, adding salt and/or hot pepper sauce, as you like. The sauce will be quite thick—perfect for spooning onto foods or using as a dip. If you prefer a thinner sauce, stir in water, one tablespoon at a time, until you have the consistency you like. The sauce may be prepared up to three days in advance. Store covered in the refrigerator and bring to room temperature before serving.

No, you're not seeing double. This is a tomatillo sauce, which is quite different from the preceding tomato sauce. They're members of the same family, but only distantly related. Tomatillos are easy to spot in Latin and specialty markets by the finely veined, loose papery wrapper in which they grow. Softness isn't a good guide to ripeness— tomatillos are pretty firm even when perfectly ready to eat. As long as they are free from soft spots and dark spots, they're good to go.

This sauce is delicious on all things grilled, especially salmon steaks, chicken thighs marinated in chiles and lime juice, and flank steak rubbed with salt and pepper. It is also a delicious dip for warm corn chips.

MAKES ABOUT 2 CUPS

SMOKIN' EXTRAS
Spicy-Cool Avocado Sauce

I can think of no better
warm-weather dinner
than smoked chicken
thighs or smoked and
grilled skirt steak with
this delicious sauce. It's
spicy, tart, and a little
sweet—all the flavors I
like best with smoked
foods. Start the meal
with some Smoky-Spicy
Salsa (page 21) and
warm corn chips, or
the Eastern Shore
Peel 'n' Eat Shrimp
on page 35. Try the
avocado sauce with
grilled foods, too.

MAKES ABOUT 2 CUPS

1 ripe, but not mushy, Hass
avocado

4 to 5 teaspoons fresh lime
juice

¼ cup sour cream

1 teaspooon hot red pepper
sauce, or to taste

Kosher salt

1. Halve the avocado and remove the pit. Scoop out the
flesh into the bowl of a food processor. Add the lime juice,
and process the avocado, stopping a couple of times to scrape
down the sides of the bowl, until the avocado is very smooth.

2. Scrape the mixture into a small bowl. Beat in the sour
cream and red pepper sauce. Season with additional hot red
pepper sauce, if you like, and salt to taste. The sauce can be
prepared up to one day in advance and refrigerated with a
piece of plastic wrap pressed directly to the surface to prevent
discoloration. Bring the sauce to room temperature before
serving.

NOTE: This makes a thick, dollopy kind of sauce with a velvety
texture. If you'd like a thinner sauce, better suited for drizzling or
dipping, beat 1 to 2 tablespoons water into the sauce just before
serving. Check the seasonings and add additional salt and pepper
sauce if desired.

Green Goddess Sauce

1 cup (packed) flat-leaf parsley, leaves only, washed and drip-dried

3 scallions, trimmed and coarsely chopped

3 anchovy fillets, or more if you like

2 tablespoons fresh lemon juice or tarragon vinegar

1 tablespoon chopped fresh tarragon, optional (especially good if you're using lemon juice in place of the tarragon vinegar)

1 cup mayonnaise

¼ cup sour cream

¼ cup very thinly sliced chives, optional

Few dashes hot red pepper sauce

1. Process the parsley, scallions, anchovies, lemon juice, and tarragon in a food processor until the parsley and scallions are very finely chopped. Stop to scrape down the sides of the work bowl once or twice.

2. Scrape the contents of the processor into a small bowl and stir in the mayonnaise, sour cream, chives, and hot red pepper sauce. The dressing is best if made a day or two before serving, but you can serve it right away. The sauce may be prepared up to a week in advance. Store covered in the refrigerator and bring to room temperature before serving.

The original green goddess blends mayonnaise with tarragon vinegar, anchovies, chives, parsley, tarragon, scallions, and garlic. I leave out the garlic, as I like to make this a day or two ahead and let its flavor develop. By that time, the garlic is too strong for me. If you like garlic, add a clove or two, very finely minced, just before you serve it. I also use lemon juice in place of the tarragon vinegar and add some chopped fresh tarragon (optional). While Green Goddess is often referred to as a dressing, this is not a pour-it-over-a-salad dressing, but a way to dress chunky seafood salads. Or serve it as a dipping sauce for the shrimp on page 140 or salmon fillets on page 134.

MAKES ABOUT 1¾ CUPS

Barbecue Sauce

This sauce is thinner and less sweet than most bottled barbecue sauces, which, in addition to the orange juice, make it perfect for brushing on smoked foods, either in the smoker or while finishing them on the grill or in the oven. (The thinner consistency also works better for pre-baking racks of spare ribs before smoking them.) If, however, you like a sweeter sauce, up the brown sugar. Or, increase the vinegar for a sharper sauce. Cut the water in half if you like a thicker sauce, and so on down the line.

MAKES ABOUT 2 CUPS

2 tablespoons vegetable oil

1 small yellow onion, finely chopped (about ⅔ cup)

¼ cup ketchup

¼ cup orange juice

3 tablespoons tomato paste

2 tablespoons light brown sugar

2 tablespoons white vinegar

Hot red pepper sauce to taste

1. Heat the oil in a heavy medium saucepan over medium heat. Stir in the onion and cook, stirring occasionally, until the onion is light golden brown, about 8 minutes.

2. While the onion is cooking, whisk the remaining ingredients and 1 cup water together in a bowl until smooth. Stir this mixture into the pan when the onions are done cooking. Bring the sauce to a boil, then adjust the heat so the sauce is barely simmering. Cover the pan and cook until the onion is completely tender, about 10 minutes. Taste and add more of any of the ingredients to balance the sauce to your taste. You may leave the sauce slightly chunky or cool it to room temperature and blend until smooth. The sauce will last up to two weeks, covered, in the refrigerator.

Best-of-the-Carolinas Barbecue Sauce

1 cup cider vinegar

⅓ cup ketchup

2 tablespoons deli-style
   mustard

2 tablespoons sugar

I teaspoon red pepper flakes

Kosher salt

Bring all the ingredients and ¾ cup water to a simmer in a medium saucepan over low heat, stirring to dissolve the sugar. Simmer until lightly thickened, about 15 minutes. Cool to room temperature. The sauce will keep in the refrigerator for up to two weeks.

Before the letters and emails start to pour in from the Carolinas, let me say one thing: This is *my* blend of the vinegary mop sauces, the mustard-based sauces and ketchupy sauces that hail from different parts of the Carolinas. All of the above are worth searching out and trying. I developed this sauce specifically for the Pulled Pork on page 170, which is also a nontraditional approach to that classic American dish. Heresy? Maybe. Delicious? Definitely.

MAKES ABOUT 2 CUPS

Brown Gravy

Smoking cooks and flavors food with a minimum of effort. You are marinating, seasoning, and saucing the foods you're smoking—simply by setting them on the smoker rack. The dips, sauces, rubs, and tips for Combo-Cooking that I offer are ways to gild the lily. So it is with this brown gravy, which is a sort of all-purpose sidekick, when serving mashed potatoes with smoked pork chops or oven-baked stuffing with turkey. If you like a thicker gravy, increase the flour to ¼ cup. I should probably call this "Tan Gravy." Browning the onion will color the gravy a little. But if you're looking for a true brown gravy, buy a bottle of Kitchen Bouquet and use it to color the finished gravy.

MAKES ABOUT 3 CUPS

3 tablespoons unsalted butter

½ cup finely diced onion

3 tablespoons all-purpose flour

3 cups homemade, or canned, reduced-sodium chicken or beef broth, hot

2 bay leaves

Kosher salt

Freshly ground black pepper

1. Heat the butter in a medium saucepan over medium heat until foaming. Stir in the onion and cook, stirring, until tender and well browned, about 12 minutes. Sprinkle the flour over the onions and stir until incorporated into the butter. Cook, stirring constantly, about 4 minutes.

2. Pour in the hot broth slowly, stirring constantly. Drop in the bay leaves and season the gravy lightly with salt and pepper. Bring to a boil, stirring constantly. Adjust the heat so the sauce is simmering and cook, stirring often, until the gravy is thick enough to lightly coat a spoon, about 10 minutes. Taste the gravy and add salt and pepper if necessary. Pick out the bay leaves and pour the gravy into a serving boat. Serve hot. The gravy can be made up to two days in advance. Pour the hot gravy into a storage container and cool it to room temperature with a piece of plastic wrap pressed directly onto the surface to prevent a skin from forming. Reheat the gravy in a heavy saucepan over low heat, adding a little broth or water if necessary to restore the gravy to its original consistency.

Smoky-Spicy Salsa

8 smoked plum tomatoes

1 large poblano chile or 3
    jalapeño chiles, stemmed
    and finely diced

½ small red onion, finely
    diced (about ¼ cup)

3 tablespoons chopped fresh
    cilantro

Kosher salt

Be prepared with an extra bag of chips—people will work through this salsa as quickly as you can put it out.

MAKES ABOUT 3 CUPS

1. Smoke the tomatoes according to the directions on page 212. Cool them to room temperature.

2. Peel off as much of the skins as will come off easily. Chop the tomatoes coarsely and toss them together with the chiles, red onion, and cilantro in a large bowl. Season with salt to taste. The salsa improves if it stands at room temperature for about half an hour before serving. You can refrigerate the salsa for up to one day. Bring it to room temperature and drain off any liquid before serving.

NOTE: Most of the "heat" in chiles is found in the seeds. Leave them in for more kick; scrape them out carefully if you like. To avoid skin irritation, wear latex gloves when handling chiles.

SMOKED CORN CHIPS

Serving warm corn chips with the salsa or dip of your choice is one of those little things that make a big difference. Smoking them not only warms them, but adds a hint of smoky flavor that goes well with just about any salsa in this book or on your pantry shelf. Pile as many chips into a 9 × 11-inch disposable aluminum foil pan as will fit into the smoker with the lid closed. Set up the smoker using 1½ tablespoons of any type of wood chips and smoke the chips at medium heat for 10 minutes. Serve them warm from the smoker. You can smoke two or three batches of chips using the same 1½ tablespoons of wood chips.

Fresh Tomato Salsa

When Bill Hodge and I ran Blue Collar Food, a Manhattan catering company, we wrote a cookbook, also called *Blue Collar Food*. This salsa recipe was in that book, with a little less cilantro. Smoked foods, as I've said before, match well with spicy, sweet, and tart flavors. For that reason I recommend using the optional lime juice in the recipe. Spoon this salsa over smoked chicken, salmon, or flank or skirt steaks. Or, use it as a dip with smoked corn chips (see page 21), warm from the smoker.

MAKES ABOUT 2 CUPS

1 large ripe, but firm, tomato, or 3 ripe plum tomatoes, cored and cut into ¼-inch dice (about 2 cups)

¼ cup very finely diced red onion

2 tablespoons chopped fresh cilantro

1 jalapeño chile, cored and finely chopped (leave the seeds in for extra heat; take them out for a milder salsa)

Kosher salt

2 to 3 teaspoons fresh lime juice, optional

Toss the tomato, onion, cilantro, and jalapeño together in a small bowl. Add salt to taste and the lime juice, if using. Let the salsa stand for 10 to 20 minutes before serving. Drain the liquid and check again for seasoning just before serving.

Mango Salsa

1 ripe mango

3 scallions (white and green parts), trimmed and sliced thinly, or ¼ cup finely diced red onion

1 jalapeño chile, cored, seeded, and finely diced

2 tablespoons coarsely chopped fresh cilantro

½ teaspoon kosher salt

1 lime

Refreshing, simple to make, and perfect with just about any seafood or poultry that emerges from your smoker. Don't make the salsa more than an hour or so before you're ready to eat, or it will get mushy.

MAKES ABOUT 1 CUP, FOUR SERVINGS

1. Peel the mango and cut the flesh from the pit. Cut the flesh into a ¼-inch dice—don't worry if they're not perfect cubes.

2. Toss the mango, scallions, jalapeño, cilantro, and salt together in a small bowl. Squeeze in lime juice to taste. Let stand 15 to 30 minutes. Taste and add more lime juice and salt, if necessary, just before serving.

Cranberry Relish

Smoked foods are complemented by tart, spicy, and sweet flavors. This very simple compote, terrific with all kinds of smoked birds from Cornish hens to turkeys, has it all. I like it made with the lesser amount of sugar, but use the larger amount if you prefer a sweeter compote. Once a strictly seasonal item, cranberries can be found in the frozen food section year-round.

MAKES ABOUT 2 CUPS

One 2-inch length peeled fresh ginger, optional

¾ to 1 cup sugar

½ cup orange juice

1 pound fresh or frozen cranberries

1. Choose the finest grater you have to grate the ginger. Hold the ginger firmly and grate it lengthwise—going with, not against, the stringy fibers—into a 2-quart saucepan. Most likely you will end up with a small clump of fibers after grating. Discard them.

2. Scrape the ginger from the grater into the pan and add the sugar and orange juice. Bring to a boil over medium heat, stirring to dissolve the sugar. Stir in the cranberries and return to a boil. Adjust the heat to a gentle boil, cover the pan, and cook until the cranberries have popped and are tender, about 5 minutes. Cool completely before serving. The compote will keep for two weeks, covered, in the refrigerator. Bring to room temperature before serving.

Rubs

Some of these rubs require a small spice grinder to get the best results. An inexpensive—around fifteen dollars—coffee bean grinder works beautifully. I don't suggest using one grinder for both rubs and coffees; sooner or later you're going to brew yourself a pot of tarragon-Kona. You can double or triple these rub recipes if you like, but only if you plan to use the remainder within two weeks. The point of grinding the herbs and spices yourself is to give them a super-fresh flavor.

HOW TO USE THESE RUBS

Some recipes in this book call for a specific rub as a way of seasoning meats or poultry bound for the smoker. In that case, simply follow the instructions in the recipe. If you'd like to experiment, choose a rub that's compatible with what you're smoking—see the rub recipes for some suggestions—and rub away. Coat the item you're smoking with a generous amount of the rub and massage the rub gently into it. When possible, allow at least several hours for the flavor to penetrate before smoking.

Lemon-Tarragon Rub

Use for chicken, vegetables, salmon, or cod.

MAKES ABOUT 2 TABLESPOONS, enough for 4 chicken breasts or fish fillets

Zest of 1 lemon

2 teaspoons chopped fresh tarragon, or 1½ teaspoons dried tarragon

1 teaspoon kosher salt

¼ teaspoon freshly ground black pepper

Grate the zest of the lemon finely into a small bowl. Stir in the tarragon, salt, and pepper. Use within an hour.

Mushroom-Herb Rub

½ cup dried mushrooms

2 teaspoons dried thyme

2 teaspoons kosher salt

½ teaspoon freshly ground
   black pepper

½ teaspoon sugar

Grind all the ingredients to a powder in a small electric spice mill.

ANOTHER *SMOKIN'* HOT TIP: An effortless and efficient way to clean a spice grinder: Toss a couple of 1-inch pieces of day-old bread into the grinder and run the motor for a few seconds. Discard the bread. The bread will wipe the container and blades of the grinder clean.

Use for chicken, pork, beef, or vegetables. You can get as fancy as you like with the dried mushrooms. Porcini or chanterelles are a couple of high-end choices. Or do what I usually do— look for dried white button mushrooms, which are available in many supermarkets.

**MAKES ABOUT
3 TABLESPOONS,**
enough to rub 6 chicken breasts, 4 pork chops, fish fillets/steaks, or small beef steaks

Southwestern Rub

use for pork, beef, or
chicken

**MAKES ABOUT
4 TABLESPOONS,**
enough for 6 chicken breasts
or fish fillet/steaks or 4 pork
chops or small beef steaks

3 whole dried cayenne chiles,
   or I teaspoon crushed red
   pepper

2 tablespoons coriander seeds

4 teaspoons cumin seeds

2 teaspoons kosher salt

Snap the stems off the dried chiles, if using them. For a milder rub, tap out and discard the seeds. Crumble the peppers into a small saucepan and add the coriander and cumin seeds. Toast the mix over low heat, stirring constantly, until the seeds are lightly browned and little wisps of smoke rise from the pan. Pour the spices onto a plate and cool them to room temperature. Grind them to a powder in a spice mill. Store the rub in an airtight jar in a cool, dark place for up to two weeks.

Rosemary-Garlic Rub

2 tablespoons dried rosemary

2 teaspoons garlic powder

2 teaspoons kosher salt

Grind all the ingredients to a powder in a spice mill. Store the rub in an airtight jar in a cool, dark place for up to a month.

Use for chicken, pork, or beef.

MAKES ABOUT 3 TABLESPOONS, enough for 6 chicken breasts or 4 pork chops or small beef steaks

appetizers
and
snacks

Smoked Trout and
Chive Cream Cheese Spread

This schmear is delicious on a bagel, spread on a crunchy cracker, or spooned into crisp celery stalks for a retro party snack. Stirring the ingredients together rather than whirring them until smooth in a food processor gives you a spread with a some texture. For an even chunkier spread, beat all ingredients except the trout together, and then gently fold in the trout.

This may be doubled easily for a larger crowd.

MAKES ABOUT 1½ CUPS

I love the look and taste of chives, and they are available in my supermarket all the time. If you don't want to fuss with chives, slice the brightest green, crispest part of a scallion very thin and use it instead.

1 smoked trout fillet

One 8-ounce container whipped cream cheese

2 scallions, trimmed and sliced very thinly

2 teaspoons fresh lemon juice

½ teaspoon kosher salt, or as needed

¼ teaspoon freshly ground white or black pepper, or as needed

3 tablespoons thinly sliced chives, optional

1. Smoke the trout according to the directions on page 138 and cool to room temperature.

2. Pick over the trout fillet, removing any fine bones or pieces of skin but leaving the trout in the largest pieces possible. Stir the trout, cream cheese, scallions, lemon juice, ½ teaspoon salt, and ¼ teaspoon pepper together gently in a mixing bowl until blended, leaving the trout in smallish pieces. Taste and stir in a little more salt and/or pepper if you like. The spread may be made up to two days in advance and stored, covered, in the refrigerator. Bring to room temperature and sprinkle the chives over the top before serving. If you're making canapés or stuffing celery with the spread, sprinkle a little of the chives over each.

Smoked Trout Fillets with Baby Greens and Horseradish Whipped Cream

2 to 3 smoked whole trout or 4 to 6 smoked trout fillets

½ cup heavy cream

½ teaspoon kosher salt, plus more for seasoning the salad

2 tablespoons mild white vinegar or fresh lemon juice

2 tablespoons bottled horse-radish

2 tablespoons finely sliced chives or chopped fresh parsley, optional

6 cups tender, not-too-bitter salad greens, like baby spinach, baby red and green romaine, or Boston lettuce—mesclun will do in a pinch—washed and thoroughly dried, preferably in a salad spinner

Freshly ground black pepper

⅔ cup olive oil

3 tablespoons fresh lemon juice

Trout and whipped cream? Once you taste this classic pairing from Eastern Europe the whole thing will make perfect sense. Match that combo up with an elegant little green salad dressed with lemon and olive oil and you have the makings of a four-star first course for your next dinner party.

MAKES 4 SERVINGS

1. Smoke the trout according to the directions on page 138. Cool them to room temperature and remove the fillets (if using whole trout) as described. Remove as many bones as possible from the fillets. The trout can be smoked up to a day in advance and refrigerated. Remove the fillets to room temperature about an hour before serving.

2. Whip the cream and ½ teaspoon salt in a chilled bowl until the cream holds soft peaks when the beaters are lifted from it. Gently stir in the vinegar, horseradish, and chives until the sauce is smooth and creamy. The sauce may be prepared up to a few hours in advance and refrigerated.

3. Just before serving, fluff the greens in a large mixing bowl and season them lightly with salt and pepper. Pour the olive oil over the greens and toss until coated. Add the lemon juice and toss until it is evenly mixed throughout the salad.

Taste the salad and add salt, pepper, lemon juice, or olive oil as you see fit. Serve the trout fillets and salad side-by-side, spooning a little of the horseradish whipped cream over the trout and passing the rest separately.

NOTE: Make sure the heavy cream is thoroughly chilled before whipping it. If you chill a metal or glass bowl and the whisk (or beaters, if using an electric mixer) for 10 to 15 minutes before whipping the cream, the cream will whip faster and hold sturdier peaks.

Eastern Shore Peel 'n' Eat Shrimp

1 tablespoon mustard seed

2 teaspoons celery seed

2 bay leaves, crumbled

1 teaspoon sweet paprika

1 teaspoon black peppercorns

12 cloves

¼ to ½ teaspoon cayenne pepper

1 pound large (21 to 25 per pound) shrimp, in the shell

2 tablespoons corn cob or alder wood chips

1. Spoon all the spices into a large resealable plastic bag. Cover the bag with a kitchen towel (so the spices don't tear the bag) and roll over the towel with a rolling pin, crushing the seasonings lightly. Pat the shrimp dry, add them to the bag, and shake them around to coat them with the spices. Refrigerate 4 to 8 hours before smoking.

2. Set up the smoker using the wood chips and smoke the shrimp according to the directions on page 140 until they are cooked throughly and firm, not springy, to the touch, about 20 minutes. Serve hot, warm, or chilled.

Beer. Very cold beer. That's the first thing I think of when these shrimp come to mind. This marinade is inspired by Old Bay seasoning—the favorite seasoning for crab or shrimp on the eastern shore of Maryland, where they know about such things. If you prefer, forgo the marinade and season the shrimp with Old Bay or your favorite seafood seasoning, but there is something nice about the crunch from an occasional mustard or celery seed that this method gives you.

MAKES 4 SERVINGS

Oysters Vanderbilt

Oysters Rockefeller was already taken, so I chose this name for these smoked oysters topped with spinach, cream, and Parmesan bread-crumbs. You can smoke and fill the oysters a day in advance. They will stay incredibly moist and fresh tasting. If you're buying shucked oysters and don't have the shells they came in, choose three small—about 3-inch—heatproof dishes and smoke, top, and broil the oysters in those.

12 smoked oysters on the half shell

2 tablespoons unsalted butter

1 large shallot, minced (about 3 tablespoons)

Kosher salt

Freshly ground black pepper

3 cups (packed) washed and stemmed fresh spinach leaves, or ¼ cup frozen chopped spinach, defrosted and drained

2 tablespoons vermouth or dry white wine, or 2 teaspoons fresh lemon juice

⅓ cup heavy cream

2 large pinches freshly grated nutmeg or bottled ground nutmeg

3 tablespoons coarse bread-crumbs (see Notes)

1½ tablespoons grated Parmesan cheese

1. In order to keep the oysters steady during broiling, line a small (about 9 × 11-inch) baking dish with rock salt or coarse sea salt (see Notes).

2. Smoke the oysters according to the directions on page 142 and cool them to room temperature.

3. While the oysters are smoking and cooling, prepare the filling. Heat the butter in a medium skillet over medium heat until foaming. Stir in the shallot, season lightly with salt and pepper, and cook, stirring often, until tender, about 4 minutes. Stir in the fresh spinach and cook until wilted and bright green, about 2 minutes. (If using frozen spinach, squeeze out as much water as possible before adding to the pan, and cook just until heated through.) Sprinkle the vermouth over the spinach and cook until evaporated. Pour in the heavy cream, add the nutmeg, and bring to a boil. Boil until the cream is reduced by about half and thickened. While the

spinach mixture is still warm, taste it and add salt and pepper as necessary. Cool to room temperature.

4. When cool enough to handle, nestle the oysters in their shells into the salt so they are level. Spoon the spinach mixture over the oysters, dividing it evenly and spreading it with the back of the spoon to cover the entire oyster. Stir the breadcrumbs and Parmesan together in a small bowl and sprinkle the mixture over the oysters. (The oysters may be prepared to this point up to one day in advance. Cover the baking pan with plastic wrap and refrigerate. Bring refrigerated oysters to room temperature 30 minutes before broiling.)

5. Set the rack about 5 inches from the broiler and preheat the broiler. Broil the oysters until the edges are bubbling and the tops are golden brown, about 3 minutes. Rotate the pan under the broiler as necessary to brown the oysters evenly. Serve immediately.

NOTES: Using rock salt to steady clams or oysters on the half shell during broiling is an old restaurant trick. You can duplicate the steadying effect of rock salt with aluminum foil: Tear off a sheet of foil about 2 inches longer than your broiling pan. Crumple it lightly, then fit it into the bottom of the broiler pan. Press the oysters and clams into the wrinkles of the crumpled foil to keep them from tipping during broiling.

Make coarse breadcrumbs by processing day-old bread in a food processor. Alternately, look for the coarsest breadcrumbs when shopping. If you live near an Asian or specialty grocery, ask for panko, very coarse breadcrumbs used in Japanese cooking.

Smoked Clams on the Half Shell with Casino Butter

A staple of Italian-American restaurants to this day, Clams Casino combine the salty tang of hard-shell clams with sweet butter, smoky bacon, and roasted red peppers. In my version, a dab of seasoned butter bathes the tender clams with flavor after they've been smoked. This recipe makes twice as much butter as you'll need for two dozen clams. Freeze the other half for your next batch of Clams Casino, or put a dollop on Cod or Haddock Fillets (page 135) hot from the smoker. If your clam-shucking skills aren't up to snuff, ask your fishmonger to shuck the clams and save the shells for you.

MAKES 4 SERVINGS

6 tablespoons unsalted butter, at room temperature

4 slices thick-cut bacon, cooked until crisp, and finely chopped

3 tablespoons minced roasted red pepper, either prepared at home (see page 54) or bottled

2 tablespoons chopped fresh flat-leaf parsley

2 teaspoons fresh lemon juice

I teaspoon Worcestershire sauce

½ teaspoon freshly ground black pepper

24 smoked littleneck or other small, hard shell clams on the half shell

I tablespoon maple, alder, or cherry wood chips

1. To make the casino butter, beat the butter, bacon, red pepper, parsley, lemon juice, Worcestershire, and black pepper together in a small bowl. The butter can be prepared up to three days in advance and refrigerated or frozen for up to 1 month. Bring the butter to room temperature about 1 hour before smoking the clams. The butter should be very soft so it melts easily when spooned onto the clams.

2. Line the bottom of a disposable 9 × 11-inch aluminum foil tray with an even ½-inch layer of rock salt. Nestle the clams on their half shells into the salt to keep them level during smoking. (See Notes on page 37.)

3. Set up the smoker using the wood chips and smoke the clams according to the directions on page 4 until they are cooked through and tinged with brown, about 12 minutes after closing the top.

4. Remove the smoker lid and drop about ½ teaspoon of the butter onto each clam. Let them sit a minute until the butter starts to melt, then transfer them carefully to serving plates or a warm platter. Serve immediately.

Smoked Salmon Pâté

Two 8-ounce smoked salmon
    fillets

10 tablespoons (1¼ sticks)
    unsalted butter, at room
    temperature

2 medium leeks, trimmed
    and cleaned (see
    page 61) and cut
    into ½-inch slices
    (about 2½ cups)

Kosher salt

Freshly ground black pepper

½ cup finely chopped fresh
    dill

1 tablespoon fresh lemon
    juice

Elegant sounding but absolute simplicity to pull off, this is a surefire party or brunch hit. Serve with whole-wheat crackers, thin slices of seven-grain bread cut into triangles, or Pumpernickel Melba Toasts (page 44). Leftovers freeze beautifully.

MAKES ONE 8-INCH ROUND, ABOUT 20 APPETIZER SERVINGS

1. Smoke the salmon fillets according to the directions on page 134 and cool them to room temperature.

2. Heat 2 tablespoons of the butter in a medium skillet over medium-low heat. Stir in the leeks, season them lightly with salt and pepper, cover the skillet, and cook until tender, about 10 minutes. Check the leeks from time to time, stir them and lower the heat if any of the leeks start to brown. Scrape the leeks into a bowl and cool to room temperature. While the leeks are cooling, lightly oil a 4-cup soufflé dish or loaf pan.

3. Flake the salmon, checking for and discarding bones, skin, and the grayish fatty layer next to the skin as you go. Add the flaked fish to the leeks in the bowl. Toss the leeks and salmon together with the dill and lemon juice. Scrape the salmon mixture into the bowl of a food processor. Cut the remaining 8 tablespoons of the butter into small pieces and add it to the salmon mix. Process, stopping the machine to scrape down the sides of the bowl a few times, until the salmon mixture is smooth with flecks of leek and dill running through it. Taste and add salt and/or pepper if necessary.

4. Scrape the mixture into the prepared dish. Tamp it lightly to make sure there are no air spaces, then smooth the top into an even layer. Cover the top with plastic wrap and refrigerate for at least eight hours, or up to two days. Bring to room temperature one hour before serving. If you like, unmold the pâté onto a serving plate by immersing the container of pâté up to its edge in a large bowl of hot water for about 3 minutes. (The time it takes to loosen the pâté from its mold depends on the material the mold is made of and the temperature of the water.) Run a thin-bladed knife along the inside edges of the container to free the sides. Invert the pâté onto the plate. If it doesn't slip out in a few seconds, re-immerse the container and try again. Serve immediately.

Portuguese-Inspired Clam and Sausage Roast

3 links (about 8 ounces) smoked hot Italian sausages (page 169), sliced ½ inch thick

2 dozen littleneck or other hard-shell clams

2 tablespoons cornmeal or flour

3 tablespoons olive oil

2 medium yellow onions, sliced ½ inch thick

4 garlic cloves, sliced thin

½ cup dry white wine

¼ cup chopped fresh flat-leaf parsley leaves

Whoever first thought to combine spicy sausages with briny clams should be inducted into the Good Food Hall of Fame. My take on this classic includes smoked Italian hot sausages and plenty of onions. With some boiled rice this becomes a meal. This "roast" is done entirely on top of the stove.

MAKES 6 APPETIZER OR 2 MAIN COURSE SERVINGS

1. Smoke the sausages according to the directions on page 4. The sausages may be smoked up to 1 day in advance, wrapped in plastic, and stored in the refirgerator.

2. Scrub the clams under cold running water to remove as much sand and dirt as possible. Fill a medium bowl with enough cold water to cover the clams. Stir in the cornmeal. Add the clams and swish them around a bit. Refrigerate the clams in the water for 2 hours, swishing two or three times.

3. Drain the clams thoroughly in a colander. Heat the oil in a 5 or 6-quart Dutch oven or heavy pot. Stir in the onions and garlic. Cook, stirring often, until the onions are softened and lightly browned, about 8 minutes. Stir in the sliced sausages and cook until heated through, about 2 minutes. Pour in the wine, increase the heat to high and bring to a boil. Cook until reduced by about half. Add the clams. Cover the pot and cook, shaking the pot occasionally, just until the clams open, about 6 minutes. Scatter the parsley over the clams and serve immediately, either from the pot or spooned into warm bowls.

Beef Jerky

Technically and traditionally, beef jerky isn't smoked, but allowed to air-dry slowly. However, the drying process was often given a boost by hanging the strips of meat over a smoldering fire. So, when adapting the process for jerky to a stovetop smoker, I start with a small amount of wood and low heat and finish with a lengthy drying process that takes place in the oven, not around a campfire.

MAKES ABOUT 6 SERVINGS

2 tablespoons kosher salt

2 tablespoons light or dark brown sugar

I pound lean top or bottom round of beef, cut into ¼ × ½ × 3-inch strips (see Note)

I tablespoon oak, mesquite, hickory, or cherry wood chips

1. Stir the salt and sugar together in a small bowl. Toss the beef strips in the marinade. Refrigerate, covered with plastic wrap, for about 6 hours, tossing several times.

2. Drain the beef thoroughly in a colander but do not rinse it or pat it dry. Lay the beef strips on the smoking rack, making sure there is space between each. Set up the smoker using the wood chips and smoke the beef according to the directions on page 4, but reducing the heat to medium-low once the lid of the smoker is closed, for 30 minutes.

3. While the beef is smoking, set the oven to "Warm" or 200°F.

4. After the beef is done smoking, transfer the beef to a baking sheet. Oven-dry the beef until it is leathery but still slightly pliable, about 4 hours. Leave on the rack in the oven to cool.

5. Store the jerky at room temperature in an airtight container or resealable plastic bag. Jerky will last indefinitely.

NOTE: When buying beef to make jerky, choose a piece that is about 3 inches long and fairly thin. It will be easier to make strips of the right size. First, cut with the grain into ¼-inch strips. Lay the strips flat and cut them lengthwise into ½-inch or so widths. Finally, if necessary, cut the strips to about 3 inches in length. Don't worry if the pieces are irregular—that is part of the fun of making your own jerky. Do, however, make sure they are no thicker than ¼ inch or they won't dry properly.

Smoky Chicken Liver Mousse with Pumpernickel Melba Toasts

Smoking chicken livers adds richness. You can get away with using less butter than you would in a traditional mousse. Pumpernickel melba toasts pair beautifully with the mousse, but you may substitute hearty crackers or store-bought melba.

MAKES 6 SERVINGS

1 pound chicken livers

2 cups milk

Kosher salt

Freshly ground black pepper

2½ tablespoons cherry, alder, or oak wood chips

2 tablespoons vegetable oil

4 tablespoons unsalted butter

1 large yellow onion, diced very fine (about ⅔ cup)

2 tablespoons port, Madeira, or sherry

2 tablespoons finely chopped fresh flat-leaf parsley, optional

1 loaf day-old, dense-textured pumpernickel bread, unsliced

Chopped toasted pistachios, walnuts, or hazelnuts, optional

1. Trim as much fat and connective tissue as possible from the livers (you'll find most of both where the two lobes of the liver meet), dropping the livers into a small bowl as you work. Pour the milk over them, cover with plastic wrap, and refrigerate for 4 to 24 hours.

2. Drain the livers and pat them as dry as you can with several changes of paper towels. Season all sides of the livers generously with salt and pepper and arrange them side-by-side in a perforated 8 × 11-inch aluminum foil pan.

3. Set up the smoker using the wood chips and smoke the livers according to the directions on page 6 until just a trace of pink remains at the center and the livers feel slightly springy and not too firm to the touch, about 12 minutes. Remove the smoker from the heat and let stand, covered, for 5 minutes. Lift the livers with tongs to a plate and cool them to room temperature.

4. While the livers are smoking and cooling, heat the oil and 1 tablespoon of the butter in a medium skillet over medium-low heat until the butter is foaming. Stir in the onion, season lightly with salt and cook, stirring often, until tender and golden brown, about 15 minutes. Scrape into a small bowl and stir in the port and parsley.

5. Grind the livers in a food processor fitted with the metal blade until they are very finely chopped. Scrape the onion mixture into the food processor and add the remaining 3 tablespoons butter, cut into small pieces. Process until the mousse is smooth but tiny bits of the onion are still visible. Scrape the mixture into a small serving bowl and refrigerate at least one day, or up to three days. Bring the mousse to room temperature at least 1 hour before serving.

6. To make the toasts (up to 4 hours before serving), preheat the oven to 350°F. If necessary, cut the bread so one face of the loaf is no more than about 3 inches across. With a bread knife, cut the trimmed loaf into very thin slices with a gentle sawing motion, arranging the slices on a baking sheet as you go. Bake the bread until crisp, about 6 minutes. The edges will probably curl up as the bread toasts; that is fine. Cool the toast to room temperature.

7. To serve, scatter the toasted nuts, if using, over the mousse and serve with the pumpernickel melba toasts.

Smoked Chicken and
Black Bean Quesadillas

Quesadillas are lightning-fast to put together, can be prepared in advance, and are universally loved. In other words, they are ideal for entertaining, especially larger groups.

Make life easy by using canned black beans and bottled roasted red peppers. (Make sure they are, in fact, roasted.) Those not labeled fire-roasted or flame-roasted are, most likely, steamed to remove the skin and

2 cups shredded smoked chicken thighs or smoked chicken breasts

1 large red bell pepper, roasted and peeled (see page 54), and cut into ¼-inch dice, or ¾ cup diced (¼-inch) bottled roasted red peppers, optional

Eight 10-inch flour tortillas

4 cups grated Monterey Jack or mild Cheddar cheese (about 8 ounces)

One 15-ounce can black beans, thoroughly drained

Draining the beans and blotting the peppers dry before putting the quesadillas together will prevent the tortillas from getting soggy. If your tortillas are a little damp after storing them, don't worry, the heat from the fire will dry them out.

1. Smoke the chicken according to the directions on page 96 or 94 and cool to room temperature. When cool, shred the chicken coarsely into pieces about $\frac{1}{2} \times 1$ inch. If using thighs, discard the fat and cartilage as you go.

2. Blot the peppers dry with paper towels. Arrange four of the tortillas on a work surface and divide the cheese among them, making an even layer of the cheese right up to the edges of the tortillas. Scatter the beans, roasted pepper, and chicken over the cheese, distributing them more or less evenly. Top with the remaining tortillas, pressing them down firmly to seal the quesadillas. (The quesadillas can be prepared up to one day in advance and refrigerated.)

3. Prepare a charcoal fire or heat a gas grill. Ready a cutting board and large, sharp knife or pizza cutter near the grill. Grill two of the quesadillas about 4 inches from the

heat until the underside is lightly browned and crispy, about 3 minutes. Slide the quesadillas to different parts of the grill once or twice to make sure they cook evenly. Flip the quesadillas and cook until the second side is light browned and crispy and the cheese is completely melted, about 2 minutes. Remove the quesadillas to the cutting board and let them stand a couple of minutes before cutting into 8 wedges. Repeat with the remaining quesadillas.

NOTE: If you plan to make the quesadillas more than an hour or two in advance, place a square of paper towel between each to keep them from sticking together.

will lack the subtle roasted flavor of their black-specked counterparts.

This recipe is written for grilled quesadillas, but they can be prepared just as easily in a skillet wide enough to hold them comfortably over medium-low heat, or, if you prefer, browned on a baking sheet under the broiler.

MAKES 10 APPETIZER OR 4 MAIN COURSE SERVINGS

Shredded Chicken with Peanut Sauce

Here is a twist on a Chinese restaurant standard: shredded smoked chicken (I prefer thighs) tossed with crispy snow peas and an Indonesian-style peanut sauce.

MAKES 6 FIRST COURSE OR 2 MAIN COURSE SERVINGS

2½ cups shredded skinless smoked chicken breasts or smoked chicken thighs

¼ pound snow peas

FOR THE PEANUT SAUCE

2 tablespoons vegetable oil

2 tablespoons minced peeled fresh ginger

2 garlic cloves, thinly sliced

¼ teaspoon red pepper flakes

⅓ cup smooth or chunky peanut butter

1 tablespoon soy sauce

1 tablespoon rice vinegar or mild white wine vinegar

1 teaspoon sugar

4 cups shredded iceberg or romaine lettuce

1. Smoke the chicken according to the directions on page 94 or 96 and cool to room temperature. When cool, shred the chicken coarsely into pieces about ¼-inch wide and 2 inches long. If using thighs, discard the fat and cartilage as you go.

2. Meanwhile, heat a medium saucepan of salted water to a boil. Add the snow peas and cook just until bright green, about 15 seconds. Drain and rinse the snow peas under cold water until completely cooled. Drain thoroughly and cut them lengthwise into ¼-inch strips.

3. To make the peanut sauce, heat the vegetable oil in a heavy, medium skillet over medium heat. Stir in the ginger, garlic, and red pepper flakes. Cook, shaking the pan gently, just until you can smell the garlic, but before it browns. (You'll smell the ginger first.) Scrape the seasoned oil into the bowl of a food processor fitted with the metal blade. Add the peanut butter, 2 tablespoons water, soy sauce, vinegar, and sugar and process until you have a fairly smooth sauce. Check the sea-

soning and add more of any of the sauce ingredients you like. Scrape the sauce into a medium bowl.

4. Add the chicken and snow peas and toss together gently until all the ingredients are lightly coated with sauce. The sauce should be thin and creamy enough to lightly coat the ingredients; if not add warm water one tablespoon at a time. Serve the salad on a bed of the shredded lettuce, either on individual plates or a large platter.

Phyllo Pastry Tartlets with Smoked Shrimp and Spinach Filling

Phyllo—ultra-thin sheets of dough that are brushed with butter and layered to create flaky pastry for Greek spinach pies, strudel, and the like—is available frozen in most supermarkets. Here, several layers of buttered phyllo are cut into little squares and pressed into mini-muffin tins to make golden brown, flaky cups that hold a spinach and smoked shrimp filling. This simple procedure for making flaky phyllo pastry cups is a handy

6 smoked shrimp

4 tablespoons unsalted butter, melted

2 scallions, trimmed and finely chopped

½ cup finely chopped cooked spinach, fresh or frozen

2 large eggs, well beaten

2 tablespoons light cream, half-and-half, or sour cream

2 tablespoons grated Parmesan cheese, plus more for dusting the tops

8 sheets phyllo dough, defrosted

1. Smoke the shrimp according to the directions on page 140, removing all the shells and tails first. Cool the shrimp to room temperature and chop them coarsely.

2. Heat 2 tablespoons of the butter in a medium saucepan until foaming. Stir in the scallions and cook, stirring, until wilted and bright green, about 1 minute. Stir in the spinach and cook until heated through and coated with butter. Scrape the spinach mixture into a small bowl and cool to room temperature. Fold in the shrimp, egg, cream, and 2 tablespoons Parmesan. Refrigerate the filling.

3. Preheat the oven to 375° F. Unwrap the phyllo dough and carefully remove 4 sheets. Lay them out flat on the work surface and cover them with a very lightly dampened kitchen towel. Refold the remaining phyllo sheets and return them to their plastic sleeve. Wrap the sleeve securely and tightly with aluminum foil and refreeze them immediately.

4. Remove two of the sheets from under the towel and lay them side-by-side on the work surface in front of you with the

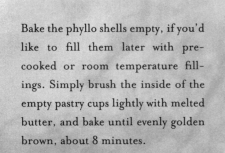

Bake the phyllo shells empty, if you'd like to fill them later with pre-cooked or room temperature fillings. Simply brush the inside of the empty pastry cups lightly with melted butter, and bake until evenly golden brown, about 8 minutes.

short sides closest to you. Lightly brush the halves of the sheets nearest you with some of the remaining melted butter. Fold the unbuttered half over the buttered portion. Brush the top of one of the folded sheets with butter and place the second folded and buttered sheet on top of it, squaring the sides to form an even rectangle of four layers. Cut the rectangle lengthwise into 3 equal strips, then crosswise into 4 equal strips to form 12 squares. Gently press each square into a compartment of a mini-muffin tin, making sure the bottom is completely lined and the edges that extend above the compartment are more or less equal on all sides. Repeat with the remaining phyllo sheets and melted butter.

5. Drop 1 tablespoon of the filling into each cup and press it down lightly. Brush the tops lightly with the remaining butter, sprinkle them with Parmesan, and bake until the pastry is golden brown and the filling is slightly firm, about 15 minutes. Cool 5 minutes before removing from the pan and serving. The spinach tartlets may be prepared up to one day in advance and refrigerated. Heat them in a 300°F oven until warmed through before serving.

one to keep in mind for parties. They can be filled and baked, as they are in this recipe, or baked empty and enriched with all manner of cooked fillings from sautéed mushrooms to Smoked Salmon Pâté (page 39).

MAKES 24

NOTES

- To defrost phyllo dough with the least amount of damage, transfer it to the refrigerator one day before you plan to work with it.
- If you prefer, start with 1 large bunch fresh spinach. Stem, wash, and dry it. Then cook it till tender, squeeze as much liquid as you can from it, and chop it fine. Measure out ½ cup and you're good to go.
- A muffin tin of the filled phyllo cups can be wrapped in aluminum foil and frozen for up to two weeks. Defrost in the refrigerator for 4 to 8 hours before baking as described above.
- The phyllo cups can be baked up to two hours in advance and warmed in a 300°F oven for 6 to 7 minutes.

World's Best Garlic Bread

This may be a little over the top to qualify as a garlic bread, but it is the best thing of this kind I've ever had. Use about sixteen cloves of garlic if you want the Parmesan cheese to share equal billing with the garlic; twice that if you want the garlic to take the lead. Choose bread that is crusty and fairly dense without being doughy. Depending on the size and shape of your loaf, you may want to cut it a tad longer or shorter than described in the recipe; just be sure the butter coats the bread in an even layer without any bare spots or thick patches. It's okay if the ends of the thin onion slices turn black during baking.

MAKES **6** SERVINGS

16 to 32 smoked garlic cloves

¼ cup grated Parmesan cheese

4 tablespoons unsalted butter, melted

3 tablespoons chopped fresh flat-leaf parsley

2 tablespoons olive oil

Kosher salt

Freshly ground black pepper

One 12-inch length of crusty baguette or Italian bread

Half a small red onion, sliced very thinly (about ½ cup)

1. Smoke the garlic according to the directions on page 219 and cool to room temperature.

2. Preheat the oven to 400°F. Blend the garlic, Parmesan, butter, parsley, and olive oil in a food processor fitted with the metal blade until the garlic is finely chopped. (Or beat all the ingredients together in a small bowl until well blended. This will leave small pieces of the garlic cloves, not necessarily a bad thing.) Taste and season with salt and pepper.

3. Split the bread lengthwise with a bread knife. Spread the garlic butter over the cut sides of both halves and set the bread buttered side up on a baking sheet. Scatter the onion slices evenly over the bread and press them gently so they stick to the garlic butter. Bake until the crust is crackling crisp and the tops are lightly browned, about 12 minutes. Cool slightly before slicing and serving.

Smoked Mozzarella

How Many? Up to four 8-ounce pieces of fresh mozzarella in one batch. If your pieces are larger than that, you may have to cut them in half crosswise so they fit in the smoker or tent the smoker with heavy-duty aluminum foil (see page 5).

How Long? 10 minutes over heat, about 15 minutes off the heat.

Which Wood? 2 tablespoons hickory or apple chips.

Start the smoker over medium heat and set the pieces of mozzarella on the corners of the rack, as far away from the central heat source as possible. When the wood starts to smoke, cover the smoker and immediately reduce the heat to low.

Check after 8 minutes. The cheese should be warm but still quite firm to the touch and have a slight tinge of color in the outer surface. As long as the cheese hasn't started to soften considerably on the bottom, leave for another 2 minutes over the heat. At that point, or if the cheese has started to soften sooner, remove the smoker from the burner and let it stand covered, 15 to 20 minutes. Remove the cheese to a plate and cool completely to room temperature.

Serve with roasted red peppers (see box on the next page), fresh basil leaves, and a drizzle of the best olive oil you can get your hands on. A pretty way to present this combination is to alternate slices of smoked mozzarella, strips of roasted peppers, and whole basil leaves, drizzling olive oil and scattering cracked black pepper and coarse salt over all.

Slice smoked mozzarella for homemade pizzas or delicious sandwiches. Cut it into smallish cubes and toss into a panful of pasta and tomato sauce at the very last second before serving.

When you smoke your own mozzarella, you won't end up with the brown outer layer you'll find in commercially smoked mozz. But you will end up with a mellow, woody flavor that lets the taste of fresh mozzarella shine through. Follow these instructions, or you'll end up with a mozzarella puddle.

Unless sodium in your diet is an issue, I suggest salted mozzarella for smoking. Start with the freshest mozzarella and smoke it as soon after it is made as you can. And smoke the mozzarella as close to serving time as possible. Refrigeration will affect the texture of a smoked mozzarella—and not in a good way. Leave the cheese at room temperature for up to three hours before serving to retain that tender, creamy texture.

TO ROAST BELL PEPPERS

Choose boxy, flat-sided peppers with thick flesh for roasting. They will blacken more evenly and quickly.

Using a gas range: Turn the flame to high. Balance the peppers on the grate over the flame and let the underside blacken completely. Turn the peppers as necessary with a long pair of tongs until all sides are evenly blackened.

Using a broiler: Position the rack about 5 inches from the broiler and preheat the broiler to its highest setting. Broil the peppers on a broiler pan, turning them as necessary, until they are completely and evenly blackened on all sides, 6 to 8 minutes.

In either case, transfer the peppers to a large bowl and cover the bowl tightly with plastic wrap. Cool completely. To peel, stand a pepper on its stem end and, working from the opposite end, pull the pepper into sections following the ridges in the pepper. Place the pepper blackened side up on a cutting board and scrape the blackened skin off with a small knife. Resist the temptation to rinse the peppers, as you will lose a lot of the flavor—the very reason you roasted them in the first place.

Eggplant Dip

One 1-pound smoked eggplant

3 tablespoons olive oil, plus more for serving, if you like

1 small yellow onion, minced (about ½ cup)

2 garlic cloves, minced

3 tablespoons chopped fresh flat-leaf parsley

Kosher salt

Lemon wedges, optional

Akin to eggplant caviar—named for its pearly texture, not its flavor—this dip (or spread or sandwich filler) pairs silky smooth eggplant with olive oil, onions, and garlic. For a different take, substitute chopped fresh cilantro for the parsley. I strongly suggest salting the eggplant slices (see page 215) before smoking them. For dipping, use toasted whole-wheat pita chips or Pumpernickel Melba Toasts (page 44).

MAKES ABOUT 1 CUP, enough for 6 people as a nibble

1. Peel the eggplant completely and smoke it according to the directions on page 215. Cool to room temperature.

2. Meanwhile, heat 3 tablespoons olive oil in a small skillet over medium heat. Add the onion and cook, stirring often, until wilted, about 4 minutes. Stir in the garlic and cook, stirring often, until the onion is golden brown, about 8 minutes. Remove from the heat and stir in the parsley.

3. Chop the eggplant fine with a knife. (I prefer this to using a food processor, which can turn the eggplant to mush.) Scrape it into a small bowl and stir in the onion mixture. Taste and add salt if necessary. If you like, squeeze the juice from a lemon wedge or two into the dip, and serve a few more wedges with the dip.

Toasted Pita Chips

Preheat the oven to 325°F. Split 2 whole-wheat pitas into two rounds each by gently pulling the outer edges apart. Cut each of the four circles into 8 triangles. Spread the triangles out on a baking sheet and bake until crisp and golden brown, about 15 minutes. Stir the pita several times as they toast so they brown evenly. Serve warm or cool. The pita chips may be made one or two days in advance, if the weather isn't too humid. Store them loosely covered at room temperature.

Not-Your-Mother's Onion Dip

This quick onion dip gets its light, clean flavor and a hint of sweetness from smoked Vidalia onions. Dip into this with potato chips or warm blue corn chips, or use as a baked potato topper or accompaniment to meat loaf.

MAKES ABOUT 3 CUPS

1 medium smoked Vidalia or other sweet onion

¾ cup sour cream

¼ cup mayonnaise

1½ teaspoons Worcestershire sauce

¼ teaspoon freshly ground black pepper

Kosher salt

1. Smoke the onion according to the directions on page 217 and cool it to room temperature.

2. Chop the onion finely. (You can do this in a food processor if you like.) Stir the sour cream, mayonnaise, Worcestershire sauce, pepper, and chopped onions together in a small bowl until blended. Season to taste with salt. Chill the dip for at least 8 hours or up to two days. Bring the dip to room temperature 1 hour before serving.

In-Flight Almonds

8 ounces (about 2 cups) whole
  almonds, peeled or
  unpeeled, as you prefer
  (a mix of the two looks
  nice)

1 teaspoon Asian sesame oil
  or vegetable oil

1 teaspoon confectioners' sugar

1 teaspoon fine sea salt

⅛ teaspoon cayenne pepper

2 tablespoons hickory wood
  chips

1. Toss the almonds together with the oil in a large bowl until coated. Sprinkle the sugar, salt, and cayenne over them while tossing until the nuts are evenly coated. Spread the seasoned almonds in an even layer over the bottom of a perforated 8 × 11-inch aluminum pan.

2. Set up the smoker using the wood chips and smoke the almonds until the nuts are toasted and the coating is glossy, about 14 minutes. Remove from the heat and cool them completely. The nuts can be stored in an airtight container for up to five days. Serve them at room temperature or warm them in a 250°F oven for 5 minutes before serving.

> If you don't have fine sea salt, measure ¼ cup kosher salt and grind in a food processor until very fine. Measure out the amount you need for this recipe and save the rest for future batches of almonds or another use.

Inspired by—but much better than—the little foil packs of almonds that now constitute an in-flight meal, these crunchy, smoky almonds are absolutely addictive. They are much better (i.e., crunchier and mellower in flavor) the next day, or they would be if there were ever any left. Start with the sugar, salt, and cayenne amounts outlined below and fine-tune the sweet/salty/spicy ratio as you go. I list hickory wood chips in the ingredients but, as always, follow your whim. As for peeled vs. unpeeled almonds, the choice is yours. The seasonings stick better to unpeeled almonds, but not everyone likes the slightly bitter flavor of unpeeled almonds. I do.

MAKES ABOUT 2 CUPS

soups
and
salads

Monster Minestrone

Simmering smoked pork in a vegetable soup was inspired by Lidia Bastianich. She simmers a piece of cured, smoked pork butt in the soup, then arranges a few slices in a soup bowl before ladling in the steaming hot minestrone. I do the same, but prefer to smoke my own pork tenderloin. If you're feeding a good-sized group, smoke two tenderloins and make the soup as described. For a smaller group, make the soup, but ladle half into storage containers after step 3. Refrigerate or freeze that half. Simmer just one smoked tenderloin in the remaining soup and go full steam ahead. Use tenderloins that were smoked a day or two in advance and refrigerated until the soup was made.

MAKES 10 SERVINGS

1 or 2 smoked pork tenderloins

⅓ cup olive oil

2 medium yellow onions, diced (about 3 cups)

2 medium leeks, optional, cleaned (see box, next page) and sliced ½ inch thick

3 medium carrots, peeled and diced (about 1½ cups)

2 stalks celery, trimmed and diced (about 1 cup)

¾ pound white or cremini mushrooms, trimmed and sliced (about 4 cups)

Kosher salt

Half a small head (about 1½ pounds) savoy cabbage, core removed, leaves shredded ½ inch thick (about 6 cups)

2 large parsnips or medium white turnips, peeled and diced (about 2 cups)

Two 46-ounce cans low-sodium chicken broth

2 small zucchini, trimmed and diced (about 2 cups)

½ pound string beans, ends trimmed, cut into 1-inch lengths (about 2 cups)

One 15-ounce can diced tomatoes

One 15-ounce can cannellini beans or red kidney beans, drained and rinsed

1 to 1½ cups frozen peas

1 cup small pasta shapes, like acini di pepe, tubetti, or orzo

Freshly ground black pepper

EXTRAS (use any or all that you like)

Pesto (page 63)

Grated Parmesan cheese

Extra virgin olive oil

Bruschetta (page 82)

1. Smoke the tenderloins according to the directions on page 163. The tenderloins may be smoked up to 2 hours in advance and stored at room temperature, or up to two days in advance and refrigerated.

2. Heat the olive oil in a 5 to 6-quart heavy pot or Dutch oven over medium heat. Add the onions, leeks, if using, carrots, celery, and mushrooms and season them lightly with salt. Cook, stirring often, until they begin to steam and sizzle, about 8 minutes. Stir in the cabbage and parsnips and cook, stirring often, until the cabbage is wilted, about 5 minutes.

3. Add the chicken broth, zucchini, string beans, tomatoes, cannellini beans, and peas. Increase the heat to high and bring to a boil. Season to taste with salt. Adjust the heat so the liquid is at a gentle boil, cover the pot, and cook until all the vegetables are tender, about 10 minutes. The soup may be prepared to this point up to three days in advance. Cool it to room temperature, then refrigerate it right in the pot. Bring to a simmer over low heat before continuing.

4. Bring a medium saucepan of salted water to a boil. Stir in the pasta and cook, stirring occasionally, until al dente, 6 to 10 minutes, depending on the pasta shape you choose. Drain the pasta and stir it into the soup. (Note: If you plan to refrigerate or freeze all or part of the soup, do so before adding the pasta.)

5. After stirring the pasta into the water, slip the tenderloins into the soup. Cook until they are heated through, about 15 minutes.

TO CLEAN LEEKS

Cut off the root end of the leek. All of the light green and white parts of the leek are used for cooking, so it is best to remove the dark green part while leaving the white and light green parts intact. Hold the leek by the root end and, with a sturdy sharp knife, scrape away the tougher outer leaves. It is more like whittling than cutting; you should end up with a leek that looks like a sharpened pencil with a medium-green tip. Cut the trimmed leek in half lengthwise and rinse each half under cool running water to remove the grit that lodges between the layers. The leeks are now ready to cut and cook as needed.

6. Taste the soup and add salt and pepper if you like. Remove the pork tenderloin(s) to a cutting board. Slice thinly and arrange a few slices over the bottom of each soup bowl. Ladle the hot soup over the pork and serve immediately. Pass whichever of the extras you choose separately at the table, allowing guests to help themselves.

Pesto

½ cup extra virgin olive oil

¼ cup pine nuts or walnuts

2 garlic cloves

4 lightly packed cups fresh
   basil (about 4 ounces),
   stems removed

¼ cup grated Parmesan
   cheese

Kosher salt

MAKES ABOUT ⅔ CUP

Pour the olive oil into a food processor or blender and toss in the pine nuts and garlic. Process until the nuts are finely chopped. Lightly pack about half the basil into the bowl or blender jar and process until coarsely chopped. Add the remaining basil and continue processing until the basil is finely chopped. You don't want a purée, but a sauce with some texture. Stir in the Parmesan and salt to taste. If you're not serving the pesto immediately, store it in the refrigerator with a small piece of plastic wrap pressed directly on the surface to prevent discoloration. The pesto can be stored for up to three days in the refrigerator or frozen for up to one month.

Smoked Eggplant Soup

Use vegetable broth in place of the chicken broth for a vegetarian first course.

MAKES 6 SERVINGS

1 medium smoked Italian eggplant (about ¾ pound)

Kosher salt

3 tablespoons olive oil

2 medium yellow onions, diced ¼ inch (about 2½ cups)

4 garlic cloves, thinly sliced

1½ tablespoons tomato paste

5 cups homemade or canned reduced-sodium chicken broth

Freshly ground black pepper

Fresh lemon juice

If you'd like to enrich this lean, flavorful soup a bit, swirl 3 or 4 tablespoons of olive oil, butter, or light cream into the soup just before serving.

1. Peel the eggplant. Slice, salt, and smoke the eggplant according to the directions on page 215. Cool the eggplant slices to room temperature and chop them coarsely.

2. Heat the olive oil in a 5 to 6-quart heavy pot over medium-low heat. Stir in the onions and garlic and cook, stirring often, until tender and golden brown, about 12 minutes. Stir in the tomato paste and cook, stirring, until you can smell it and it turns brick red, about 2 minutes. Add the eggplant and stir a minute or two.

3. Pour in the chicken broth, increase the heat to high, and bring to a boil. Adjust the heat so the soup is simmering and cook 10 minutes. Cool about 20 minutes.

4. Working in batches, process the soup in a food processor fitted with the metal blade to a fairly smooth consistency. (You can use a blender, but cool the soup completely first and blend using short on/off pulses, so you don't give the

soup a frothy texture.) Return the soup to the pot. The soup may be prepared to this point up to two days in advance and refrigerated. Bring to a simmer over low heat and check the seasonings, adding salt, pepper, and lemon juice to taste just before serving.

Mexican Tortilla and Smoked Corn Soup

What's nice about this soup is that it can be tailored to each person's own taste. In this case, what arrives at the table is a brothy soup, studded with golden kernels of smoked corn and diced tomato. You supply the other ingredients in bowls of various sizes, allowing people to add what they wish. Serve the

FOR THE BROTH

4 ears smoked corn on the cob

Two 46-ounce cans reduced-sodium chicken broth

2 large tomatoes, cored, seeded, and chopped

Kosher salt

Freshly ground black pepper

FOR THE STIR-INS

Toasted Tortilla Strips (recipe follows)

4 cups shredded smoked chicken thighs, smoked chicken breasts, or any leftover smoked or roasted chicken (minus skin and gristle)

6 scallions, trimmed and sliced thinly

About 1 cup cilantro leaves, no stems, washed and patted dry

2 limes, cut into large wedges

1 large, ripe Hass avocado

Why use reduced-sodium chicken broth and then add salt? One of the first things I learned when I started cooking was you can put salt in something, but you can't take it out. Some brands of chicken broth are loaded with salt, which doesn't leave you an option. (Who knows? Maybe your shredded chicken or tortilla strips are salty.) By starting with as little salt as possible, you can feel your way along step by step and keep your seasoning on track.

1. Smoke the corn according to the directions on page 214. When cool enough to handle, remove the kernels by holding each ear firmly with one hand and scraping the kernels from the cob with a short, sharp knife. Remove as much of the kernels as you can without cutting into the cob. Separate the kernels and set them aside. The corn may be smoked and stripped up to one day in advance. All the stir-ins, with the exception of the avocado, may be prepared a day in advance as well. Refrigerate all ingredients until you're ready to serve the soup.

2. Stir the chicken broth, tomatoes, and smoked corn kernels together in a heavy 5-quart pot. Bring to a boil over medium heat. Check the seasoning, adding salt and pepper as necessary.

3. While the soup is coming to a boil set each of the stir-in ingredients in a separate bowl and prepare the avocado. Peel the avocado and cut it into 1-inch dice, squeezing one or two of the lime wedges over the pieces as you go. This will prevent the avocado from turning brown.

4. Ladle the soup into warm bowls at the table and pass the stir-in ingredients so each person can doctor the soup as he or she likes. Keep the soup hot on the stove for those who'd like seconds.

soup piping hot in warm bowls. If you're having people to dinner who haven't met each other before, there is an instant sense of community as they pass the stir-ins back and forth across the table.

MAKES **6** SERVINGS

Toasted Tortilla Strips

Preheat the oven to 350°F. Cut four yellow or white corn tortillas in half, then crosswise into ½-inch strips. Spread the strips out on a baking sheet. Drizzle about 1 teaspoon olive or vegetable oil into the palm of your hand, rub your hands together lightly, then toss the tortilla strips to coat them very lightly with oil. Bake, stirring once about halfway through, until the tortilla strips are crispy and golden brown, 6 to 7 minutes.

Turkey-Mushroom-Barley Soup

The next time you smoke a turkey (page 101) or two chickens (page 92), save the carcass(es) and make this delicious soup. Chances are you'll be able to pick all the meat you need from the bones before you make the broth. I freeze half of this soup, which I do before adding the barley.

MAKES ABOUT 2½ QUARTS
(6 SERVINGS)

FOR THE BROTH

1 smoked turkey carcass or two smoked chicken carcasses, including wings, if possible

1 medium yellow onion, cut in half

1 carrot, peeled and cut in half

1 celery stalk, trimmed and cut in half crosswise

6 garlic cloves

2 bay leaves

FOR THE SOUP

¼ cup vegetable oil

1 large yellow onion, diced (about 2 cups)

1 large carrot, peeled and diced (about ½ cup)

2 celery stalks, trimmed and diced (about ¾ cup)

Kosher salt

1 pound white or cremini mushrooms, wiped clean and sliced ½ inch thick

1 cup pearl barley

½ pound string beans, cut into ½-inch lengths (about 1 cup), optional

Freshly ground black pepper

¼ cup chopped fresh flat-leaf parsley

1. To make the broth, pick as much meat as you can from the turkey bones, shredding it into rough 1-inch pieces as you go. Refrigerate the meat. Choose a pot into which the turkey bones fit comfortably and pour in enough cold water to cover the bones completely. Add the halved onion, carrot, celery stalk, garlic, and bay leaves. Bring to a boil over high heat, skimming off the foam that rises to the surface. Boil 2 minutes, then adjust the heat so the liquid is simmering. Cook 2 to 3 hours, occasionally skimming the surface.

2. Ladle the broth through a fine strainer into a large bowl. Reserve 2 quarts of the broth and save the remaining

broth for other soups. The broth may be made up to three days in advance and refrigerated, or frozen for up to two months.

3. To make the soup, heat the vegetable oil in a heavy 5-quart pot over medium heat. Stir in the diced onion, carrot, and celery and season them lightly with salt. Cook, stirring often, until they are lightly browned, about 10 minutes. Stir in the mushrooms and cook until wilted, about 5 minutes.

4. Pour in the reserved 2 quarts broth and bring to a boil. Stir in the barley and string beans. Season the soup with salt and pepper and return the soup to a boil. Adjust the heat so the soup is at a lively simmer and cook until the barley is tender, about 25 minutes.

5. Stir in the reserved turkey meat and the parsley, and season the soup with salt and pepper, if necessary. Serve hot.

Split Pea and Smoked Turkey Soup

Odd as it may sound, this soup will be transformed by serving it with two kitchen pantry staples: lemon wedges and a piece of good Parmesan. Pass the cheese with a grater and let people help themselves as they like.

MAKES 6 GENEROUS SERVINGS

2 tablespoons olive or vegetable oil

2 tablespoons unsalted butter

1 large yellow onion, diced (about 2½ cups)

3 medium carrots, peeled and diced (1 generous cup)

2 celery stalks, trimmed and diced (about ¾ cup)

Kosher salt

One 46-ounce can reduced-sodium chicken broth, plus additional broth or water, if needed

3 whole smoked turkey wings (page 106) or 6 smoked turkey wing segments

1 pound green or yellow split peas

Freshly ground black pepper

1. Heat the oil and butter in a 5-quart heavy pot or Dutch oven over medium heat until the butter is foaming. Stir in the onion, carrots, and celery, season with salt and stir until the vegetables start to sizzle, about 5 minutes. Adjust the heat to low, cover the casserole and cook, stirring occasionally, until the vegetables are tender, about 15 minutes.

2. Pour in the can of chicken broth, add the turkey wings, and bring to a boil over medium heat. Adjust the heat so the broth is simmering, cover the pot, and cook 30 minutes.

3. Stir in the split peas and add enough chicken broth or water to cover them completely, if necessary. Bring to a simmer, cover the pot and cook until the split peas are tender and the turkey meat begins to fall from the bone, about 35 minutes. Check the soup occasionally as it cooks; there should be enough liquid to barely submerge the split peas as they cook. If necessary, add more chicken broth or water as the soup cooks. If the turkey wings are done before the split peas, pull them out and let them stand at room temperature until you need them.

4. When the split peas are tender, remove the turkey wings if you haven't already done so. At this point you have some options as to how to serve the soup: either leave it as is if you like soup with a chunky texture or, carefully, whisk the soup to break up the peas and give the soup a somewhat smoother texture. Season to taste with salt and pepper. Also, you can serve the turkey wings as is—one section in the bottom of each bowl—or pick the meat from them, discarding the skin and bones, and stir the meat back into the soup. Serving the wings whole is kind of messy, but fun. Shredding the meat is a little more elegant—better for a dinner party or if you plan to freeze a portion of the soup. Serve the soup in warm bowls.

Smoky Mussel Chowder

Here is a chowder that is lighter than expected, with built-in flexibility: you can make it like a traditional chowder—chock full of potatoes, or substitute parsnips for the potatoes. Their earthy flavor pairs beautifully with the briny-smoky flavors of the mussels. Or take the chowder in a different direction altogether with the addition of white beans in place of the potatoes or parsnips. Try the "Jigsaw" Croutons (page 89) if you like a little crunch with your chowder.

MAKES 6 CUPS (ABOUT 6 FIRST COURSE OR 2 MAIN COURSE SERVINGS)

2 pounds smoked mussels

3 tablespoons unsalted butter

2 medium leeks, cleaned (see page 61) and thinly sliced (about 2½ cups)

2 small celery stalks, preferably with leaves, thinly sliced (about ½ cup)

Kosher salt

4 cups homemade or canned reduced-sodium chicken broth

1 pound Idaho or Yukon gold potatoes, peeled and diced ⅓-inch (about 2 cups; see Variations)

¼ cup chopped fresh flat-leaf parsley

1 cup light cream or half-and-half

Freshly ground white or black pepper

Paprika, optional

1. Smoke the mussels according to the directions on page 141. When the mussels are cool enough to handle, pluck them from their shells. If necessary, remove any traces of the mussels' beards—the wiry material that protrudes from about halfway down the flat side of the mussel—as you go. Set the mussels aside while you continue. The mussels may be smoked, plucked, and refrigerated up to one day in advance.

2. Heat the butter in a heavy 3-quart saucepan over medium heat until bubbling. Stir in the leeks and celery and season them lightly with salt. Cook, stirring, until the leeks are tender, about 6 minutes.

3. Pour in the chicken broth, increase the heat to high and bring to a boil. Stir in the potatoes and adjust the heat so the liquid is simmering. Season with salt and simmer until the potatoes are tender, about 8 minutes.

4. Stir in the parsley and mussels. Pour the cream into a heatproof bowl and slowly add a few ladlefuls of the hot soup, stirring constantly. Pour the cream mixture into the pot and season with salt, if necessary, and pepper. Serve immediately in warmed soup bowls, sprinkling the soup with paprika if you like.

VARIATIONS: Substitute an equal amount of parsnips, peeled and cut as described above, or one 15-ounce can of white beans, drained and rinsed, for the potatoes.

Smoked Chicken, Pecan, and Gruyère Salad

There are times when a simple green salad with an olive oil and vinegar dressing hits the spot, yet there are times when I want something unique, like here. There's something for every taste bud in this salad—tart, juicy apples; moist, smoky chicken; salty-sweet toasted pecans; and sweet and sour honey-mustard dressing. Your choice of greens and cheese—Gruyère or its milder, nuttier cousin Jarlsberg—will make this salad your own. The nice thing about smoking chicken breasts is that they remain moist so you can refrigerate leftovers without them developing the texture of a corrugated cardboard box. Next time you're smoking chicken breasts, toss a couple extra ones into the smoker for this salad.

MAKES 2 SERVINGS

2 smoked chicken breasts, skin removed if necessary, chicken sliced thinly, or 2 cups shredded smoked chicken thighs

FOR THE PECANS (or substitute simple toasted pecan halves or walnut pieces)

¾ cups (about 2 ounces) pecan halves

½ teaspoon Asian sesame oil or vegetable oil

¼ teaspoon sugar

⅛ teaspoon salt

FOR THE DRESSING

1 tablespoon mayonnaise

2 teaspoons grainy or Dijon mustard

2 teaspoons white wine vinegar

1 teaspoon honey

¼ cup extra-virgin olive oil

Kosher salt

Freshly ground black pepper

FOR THE SALAD

8 cups salad greens—just about anything goes, from thinly shredded romaine leaves to baby spinach to mesclun or a mix of arugula and Boston lettuce, washed and dried thoroughly, preferably in a salad spinner

1 Granny Smith or Fuji apple

1 cup coarsely shredded Gruyère or Jarlsberg cheese (about 3 ounces)

¼ cup dark or golden raisins, optional

1. Smoke the chicken according to the directions on page 94 or 96. Cool to room temperature. The chicken may be smoked up to two days in advance and refrigerated.

2. To toast the pecans, preheat the oven to 350°F and drizzle the oil over the pecans in a small bowl, tossing to coat. Sprinkle the sugar and salt over the nuts and toss again. Spread them out on a baking sheet and bake until evenly light

golden brown, about 10 minutes. It's a good idea to stir the nuts with a wooden spoon about halfway through the toasting, so they brown evenly. Cool the pecans to room temperature. If conditions aren't too humid, you can prepare the toasted walnuts up to a day in advance. Store them at room temperature.

3. To make the dressing, whisk the mayonnaise, mustard, vinegar, and honey together in a small bowl. Pour in the olive oil while whisking constantly. Add salt and pepper to taste. This makes enough dressing for the salad ingredients outlined above. You can triple or quadruple the dressing ingredients and prepare the dressing in a food processor or blender if you like. The dressing will last about a week in the refrigerator.

4. Just before serving the salad, fluff the salad greens up in a large mixing bowl and let them stand at room temperature for about 10 minutes.

5. Cut the apple into quarters and cut out the core section from each. Cut the quarters into very thin slices—or ½-inch dice for more crunch—and scatter them over the greens along with the sliced chicken, grated cheese, and raisins. Season the salad with salt and pepper, pour the dressing over all, and toss until everything is coated with dressing. Divide between two serving bowls and serve.

NOTE: Place a damp kitchen towel between the bottom of the bowl and the work surface to steady the bowl while you're whisking the dressing. This is especially useful when whisking larger batches of this or any dressing.

Shredded Duck, Toasted Hazelnut, and Watercress Salad

Watercress, with its peppery, crisp personality, is the perfect accompaniment to rich, smoky duck. You can prepare everything you need for this salad well in advance of serving it, but wait until the last minute to bring it all together. It's the warm duck tossed with cool greens that make this such a treat. A word of advice: make sure your ground cumin is fresh. (Open the jar and take a whiff if in doubt; you should smell a clean, pleasantly sharp aroma, not a muted or musty scent.) It makes all the difference. For the best flavor possible, toast and grind the cumin seeds (see page 28) just before making the dressing. You can make this with chicken instead of duck.

MAKES 6 FIRST COURSE SERVINGS

4 smoked duck legs

½ cup hazelnuts, preferably peeled

2 bunches watercress, with thinner stems and tender, smaller leaves

½ cup olive oil, plus 2 tablespoons

3 tablespoons orange juice

½ teaspoon ground cumin

Kosher salt

Freshly ground black pepper

1. Smoke the duck legs according to the directions on page 112 and cool them to room temperature. When they are cool enough to handle, pull the meat from the bones, discarding fat and cartilage, and shredding the meat coarsely as you go. The duck can be smoked and shredded up to two days in advance.

2. Preheat the oven to 350°F. Spread the hazelnuts out on a baking sheet and toast them in the preheated oven until uniformly golden brown, about 15 minutes. Shake the pan several times as the nuts roast so they brown evenly. If necessary, remove as much of the skins as possible by rolling the warm hazelnuts in a kitchen towel. Chop the hazelnuts coarsely and set them aside. The nuts can be toasted and chopped up to a day in advance. Store them loosely covered at room temperature.

3. Trim the ends and any stems that are thicker than a strand of spaghetti from the watercress. Wash the cress in cool water and dry thoroughly in a salad spinner. Store the cress at room temperature for up to 30 minutes or in a bowl covered with a damp paper towel in the refrigerator for up to one day.

4. About 15 minutes before serving, fluff the watercress in a large mixing bowl. (Not necessary if your cress is at room temperature.) Pour ½ cup of the olive oil and the orange juice into a small container with a tight fitting lid. Add the cumin and season lightly with salt and pepper. Shake vigorously, taste again, and add salt and/or pepper if you like.

5. Heat the remaining 2 tablespoons olive oil in a large skillet over medium heat. Add the duck and cook, stirring occasionally, until the duck is heated through and just begins to brown, about 10 minutes. Remove from the heat.

6. Give the dressing a vigorous shake and pour it over the watercress. Scatter the hazelnuts over the salad, spoon the duck over the top and toss everything together until the watercress is coated and very lightly wilted. Serve immediately.

Toasted Couscous, Lamb, and Spring Vegetable Salad

Leftover smoked lamb works well with the crunchy spring vegetables in this salad, but you could just as easily use bits of leftover roasted lamb. Or, substitute smoked or roasted chicken or smoked salmon for the lamb.

MAKES 6 SERVINGS

2 cups instant couscous

2 teaspoons kosher salt, or as needed

16 medium stalks asparagus

2 cups diced (½-inch) smoked lamb chops (page 196)

3 celery stalks, trimmed and finely diced (about 1 cup)

8 red radishes, trimmed, halved, and thinly sliced

½ cup frozen peas, defrosted and drained, or fresh peas, cooked and drained

¼ cup fresh lemon juice

1 teaspoon ground cumin

½ cup extra virgin olive oil

2 tablespoons Asian sesame oil

1. Preheat the oven to 350°F. Spread the couscous out on a baking pan and toast until golden brown, about 10 minutes. Shake the pan once or twice as the couscous toasts so it browns evenly. Slide the couscous into a 3-quart heatproof serving bowl and cool to room temperature.

2. Bring a medium saucepan of salted water to a boil. Meanwhile, snap and peel the asparagus according to the directions in step 2 of the Tea-Smoked Shrimp and Asparagus Stir-Fry recipe on page 150. Cut off the tips, then cut the stalks into 1-inch lengths on the diagonal. Stir the asparagus pieces into the boiling water and cook just until bright green and crisp-tender, about 1½ minutes. Drain and cool.

3. Bring 2 cups water and 1 teaspoon of the salt to simmering in the saucepan. Pour the hot water over the couscous, give it a big stir, and cover the bowl. Let it stand, fluffing once with a fork after a couple of minutes, until the water is absorbed and the couscous is tender, about 5 minutes. Fluff the couscous with a fork and cool to room temperature.

4. Toss the lamb, asparagus, celery, radishes, and peas together with the couscous. In a separate bowl, whisk the lemon juice, the remaining 1 teaspoon salt, and the cumin together until the salt is dissolved. Whisk in the olive oil and sesame oil. Pour the dressing over salad, toss well, and let stand 20 to 30 minutes before serving. Taste for seasoning and serve at room temperature.

Smoked Corn and Black Bean Salad

There are two ways I enjoy this salad, and both are below. On its own, warm from the pan, the black bean and corn salad is the best all-around side dish for grilled anything-I-can-think-of. (Cook the scallions in oil ahead of time, rewarm them, and finish the salad in the pan right on the grill.) Tossed with tender, leafy greens—which wilt slightly when you toss them with the beans and corn—it can also complement offerings from your grill. The bean-corn-greens combination is especially good with grilled flank steak or salmon. But with the greens this salad is a light meal on its own or with whole boiled shrimp or sliced grilled chicken breasts added. Although this recipe calls for the kernels from two ears of corn,

2 ears smoked corn on the cob

3 tablespoons olive oil

3 scallions, trimmed and sliced thinly

6 slices jalapeño pepper, optional

One 15-ounce can black beans, drained and rinsed

1 ripe, medium tomato, cored and diced ½ inch

Kosher salt

Freshly ground black pepper

2 tablespoons chopped fresh cilantro

1 lime, cut in half

FOR THE GREEN SALAD VERSION

8 cups (loosely packed) mesclun or other cleaned tender, leafy greens such as shredded red or green leaf lettuce, Boston lettuce, or baby arugula

Olive oil

1. Smoke the corn according to the directions on page 214. When cool enough to handle, remove the kernels: hold each ear firmly with one hand and scrape the kernels from the cob with a short, sharp knife. Remove as much of the kernels as you can without cutting into the cob. Separate the kernels and set them aside. The corn may be smoked and stripped up to one day in advance.

2. Heat the olive oil in a large skillet over medium heat. Stir in the scallions and jalapeños, if using, and cook, shaking the pan, just until they turn bright green, about 2 minutes. Stir in the beans and cook, tossing, just until warmed through, about 1 minute. Add the tomato and corn and toss gently until warmed though, 1 to 2 minutes. Remove from the heat, season with salt and pepper, and stir in the cilantro. Squeeze in

lime juice little by little until it is as tangy as you like. Serve warm.

For the green salad version, fluff the greens up in a large bowl and season them lightly with salt and pepper before you begin the warm salad. As soon as the warm salad is seasoned to your liking, scrape it over the greens. Toss well, then add more olive oil, lime juice, and salt and pepper to taste. Serve immediately.

smoke four or more ears and try the Corn, Cheddar, and Red Onion Tortilla on page 222. You will love it.

MAKES 4 SERVINGS

Tuna and White Bean Salad

Made with either leftover bits of smoked tuna steaks or Preserved Tuna, Sicilian Style, this is a quick, delicious salad fit for a barbecue, buffet, or a topper for bruschetta (see box). In our house, it's dinner.

One 19-ounce can cannellini beans, drained and rinsed

2 cups flaked smoked tuna steaks (page 137) or drained Preserved Tuna, Sicilian Style (page 154)

Half a small red onion, very thinly sliced

3 small celery stalks, preferably from the celery hearts and with leaves attached, thinly sliced

10 cherry tomatoes, quartered

1 red or yellow bell pepper, roasted (see page 54), peeled and diced ½ inch, optional

⅓ cup extra virgin olive oil or oil from Preserved Tuna, Sicilian Style (page 154)

2 tablespoons mild red wine vinegar or fresh lemon juice

Kosher salt

Freshly ground black pepper

1 bunch tender, young arugula, stems removed, washed well and dried, optional

TO MAKE BRUSCHETTA

Cut 1-inch slices from a loaf of dense-textured country bread. Brush them lightly with olive oil and grill on a charcoal or gas grill until golden brown and crispy with charred edges. (*Bruciare* means "to burn" in Italian.) Alternatively, you may toast the bread in a heavy skillet—cast iron is ideal—over medium heat until the centers are golden and the edges are lightly charred.

Toss the beans, tuna, onion, celery, tomatoes, and pepper, if using, together in a serving bowl. Pour the oil over the salad, toss lightly to coat, then add the vinegar and salt and pepper to taste. The salad is best made about half an hour before serving. Toss again and taste for seasoning before serving. If you'd like to use the arugula, toss it into the salad just before you serve it or make a ring of it on a serving platter and mound the salad in the center.

Smoky Caesar Salad

20 smoked garlic cloves

⅓ cup fresh lemon juice

2 large egg yolks

5 tablespoons grated
Parmesan cheese

3 anchovy fillets, plus more
for tossing with the salad,
if you like

1 tablespoon Dijon mustard

1 teaspoon Worcestershire
sauce

1 cup olive oil

Kosher salt

Freshly ground black pepper

2 hearts of romaine or 2
medium heads romaine
with all the darker outer
leaves stripped off

2 cups "Jigsaw" Croutons
(page 89), or store-
bought croutons

1 cup shaved Parmesan cheese
(see Note), optional

Don't be alarmed at the quantity of garlic called for in this recipe. Not only does smoking the garlic mellow and sweeten it, the process adds a mysterious, subtle flavor. Chances are, your guests won't immediately figure out the difference between this and a traditional Caesar salad, but they will know there's something unusual, and delicious, going on.

MAKES 6 SERVINGS

1. Smoke the garlic according to the directions on page 219 and cool to room temperature.

2. Combine the lemon juice and egg yolks in a very small saucepan over low heat. Cook, tilting the pan if necessary, to keep the yolks covered, until the yolks are cooked through, about 3 minutes. Pour the lemon juice and yolks into a blender and add 2 tablespoons of the grated Parmesan, 3 anchovy fillets, the mustard, Worcestershire sauce, and the smoked garlic. Blend at low speed until smooth. With the motor running, pour in the olive oil in a thin steady stream until it is all incorporated and the dressing is smooth. Taste the dressing and season with salt and pepper, as necessary. The dressing may be made up to two days in advance. Bring to room temperature an hour or so before serving the salad.

3. Remove the tips of the romaine leaves and trim any wilted or yellow leaves. Cut the heads in half lengthwise, cut out the cores, then cut the romaine into 2-inch pieces. Wash

the lettuce and spin it dry in a salad spinner. The greens may be cleaned and refrigerated in a plastic bag up to a day in advance. Bring refrigerated greens to room temperature about 30 minutes before serving them.

4. Toss the romaine and dressing together in a large serving bowl. Add the remaining 3 tablespoons of the grated Parmesan and toss again. Taste and season the salad with salt and pepper if necessary. Scatter the croutons, shaved Parmesan, if using, and additional anchovy fillets, if using, over the salad. Give the salad a big, gentle toss and serve.

NOTE: To shave Parmesan, hold a chunk of Parmesan firmly in one hand and with the other, shave off thick shards with a vegetable peeler.

Bow Tie Pasta Salad with Smoked Shrimp and Cherry Tomatoes

1½ teaspoons kosher salt, plus more for cooking the pasta and seasoning the salad

¾ pound medium (about 35 per pound) smoked shrimp, peeled and deveined

⅓ cup extra virgin olive oil, plus 2 teaspoons

Freshly ground black pepper

1½ tablespoons alder, cherry, or apple wood chips

1 pint cherry tomatoes, quartered

30 large basil leaves, shredded ¼ inch (about ½ cup)

1 pound bow tie (farfalle), or penne rigati pasta

2 to 3 tablespoons red or white wine vinegar

Pasta salad should never see the inside of a refrigerator. Chilling pasta salad makes it clumpy, mutes the flavor, and turns the pasta mushy—the death of a good pasta salad. Make this simple and fresh-tasting salad no more than 30 to 45 minutes before you plan to serve it.

MAKES 6
MAIN COURSE SERVINGS

1. Bring a large pot of salted water to a boil.

2. Meanwhile, toss the shrimp, 2 teaspoons of the olive oil, ½ teaspoon of the salt, and a generous pinch of pepper together in a small bowl until the shrimp are evenly coated with seasoning. Set up the smoker using the wood chips and smoke the shrimp according to the directions on page 140 until they are bright pink and opaque in the center, about 15 minutes.

3. While the shrimp are smoking, toss the cherry tomatoes, remaining ⅓ cup olive oil, the basil, 1 teaspoon salt, and pepper to taste together in a large bowl. When the shrimp are done smoking and still warm, toss them together with the dressed tomatoes. Let stand while cooking the pasta.

4. Stir the pasta into the boiling water. Cook, stirring occasionally, until the pasta is al dente, about 10 minutes. Drain the pasta in a colander and run it under cool water just until it stops steaming. Bounce the pasta gently in the colan-

der to remove as much water as possible. Toss the pasta together with the seasoned tomatoes and shrimp. Sprinkle the vinegar over the salad and taste. Let stand about 30 minutes, tossing and checking the seasoning occasionally. Serve at room temperature.

NOTE: Stir pasta gently until the water returns to a boil to prevent it from sticking or clumping. Once the water is boiling, you need stir it only occasionally.

Orzo Salad with Smoked Mozzarella, Broccoli, and Garlic Chips

8 ounces smoked mozzarella

½ pound (about 1¼ cups) orzo

1 stalk broccoli
   (about 8 ounces)

¼ cup olive oil, or as needed

8 garlic cloves, sliced

Kosher salt

8 sun-dried tomato halves,
   preferably loose rather
   than oil-packed

½ cup shredded fresh basil
   leaves

2 tablespoons red wine
   vinegar

Freshly ground black pepper

Like the bow tie pasta salad that precedes this—or any pasta salad for that matter—this should be made no more than an hour before you plan to serve it. You can, however, toast the orzo, soak the sun-dried tomatoes, and cook the garlic and broccoli several hours in advance and then put the salad together about half an hour before you serve it.

MAKES 6
SIDE DISH SERVINGS

1. Smoke the mozzarella according to the directions on page 53. Cool to room temperature, then cut into ½-inch cubes.

2. Preheat the oven to 350°F. Spread the orzo out on a baking sheet and toast until golden brown, about 12 minutes. Stir the orzo once or twice as it bakes so it browns evenly.

3. Cut the florets from the broccoli and chop them coarsely. Peel the stems and cut them into ¼-inch dice. Heat ¼ cup olive oil in a medium (about 9-inch) skillet and add the garlic. Cook, shaking the pan occasionally, just until the garlic starts to brown. Scoop out the toasted garlic slices with a slotted spoon and drain them on paper towels.

4. Add the broccoli to the pan and season it lightly with salt. Reduce the heat to medium-low and cook, stirring often, until the broccoli is very tender, 12 to 15 minutes. Scrape into a mixing bowl.

Choose broccoli with smooth, thick stalks. They will be easier to peel and dice.

5. While the broccoli is cooking, soak the sun-dried tomatoes: pour enough hot water over the tomatoes in a bowl to cover them completely. Let stand until softened, but not mushy, 5 to 10 minutes, depending on your tomatoes. Drain them and dice them ¼-inch. (This is not necessary if using oil-packed sun-dried tomatoes.) Toss them together with the broccoli.

6. Bring a medium saucepan of salted water to a boil. Stir in the orzo. Cook, stirring occasionally, until the orzo is al dente, about 8 minutes. Drain in a colander and rinse under cold water just until the pasta stops steaming. Drain completely.

7. Add the orzo, mozzarella, and basil to the broccoli and sun-dried tomatoes. Sprinkle the vinegar over the salad and toss again. Taste the salad. There should be enough oil from the broccoli to balance the vinegar so the salad isn't too tart. If not, add a tablespoon or so of oil and toss again. Season to taste with salt and pepper. The salad is best if made about 30 minutes in advance. Toss, check the seasonings and add more of anything you like just before serving. Scatter the garlic chips over the top and serve.

"Jigsaw" Croutons

Dense-textured Italian or French bread, sliced about ¼ inch thick

Olive oil

Grated Parmesan cheese, optional

Preheat the oven to 350°F. Brush both sides of the bread slices lightly with olive oil and set them on a baking sheet. Sprinkle the tops lightly with Parmesan, if you like. Bake until the bread is crispy and evenly golden brown, about 14 minutes. Cool the bread slices completely, then crumble them into largish, irregular pieces.

I am a texture nut. I love these croutons because their thinness makes them super-crispy and their irregular shape is more interesting than traditional cube-shaped croutons. They are also a breeze to make. Toss a handful of them into any of the salads in this chapter. Twelve slices of bread will make enough croutons for four salads, but make extra if you like. It's a good way to use day-old bread, and croutons always come in handy.

Coleslaw and Cousins

I would be remiss if I didn't include a recipe for coleslaw, the near-perfect accompaniment to most things smoked. I start you off with a basic vinegar-and-sugar slaw, then point you in a few directions—creamy, spicy, and barbecued. After that, you're free to wander off on your own.

MAKES ABOUT 3 CUPS

I small head (about 3 pounds) green cabbage

I tablespoon kosher salt, or as needed

I medium carrot, peeled and grated

3 tablespoons white vinegar, or as needed

2 tablespoons sugar, or as needed

1. Peel off any wilted or yellow leaves from the cabbage. Cut the cabbage into quarters, then cut out and discard the core. For a fine textured slaw, grate the cabbage on the coarsest side of a box grater or with the coarsest grating disk in the food processor. For a coarser texture, cut the cabbage quarters in half to make eight thin wedges. Cut the wedges crosswise into thin strips. Separate the strips before proceeding.

2. Toss the cabbage together with the salt in a colander. Let the cabbage stand until wilted, about 30 minutes.

3. Squeeze the cabbage to remove as much liquid as possible, transferring the squeezed cabbage to a large bowl as you go. Add the carrot, 3 tablespoons vinegar, and 2 tablespoons sugar to the cabbage and toss until the sugar is dissolved. Taste the slaw and add salt, sugar, or vinegar as you like. Let stand at room temperature, tossing once or twice, about 30 minutes before serving. The slaw may be made up to one day in advance and refrigerated. In either case, check the seasoning again before serving.

CREAMY SLAW: Add ¼ cup mayonnaise and stir well.

CELERY SEED SLAW: Add 2 teaspoons celery seeds.

BARBECUE SLAW: Stir 2 tablespoons of your favorite barbecue sauce into the creamy slaw, with or without the celery seeds.

poultry

Whole Chicken

How Many? One or two small fryers (about 2½ pounds each) or one large roaster (up to 5½ pounds) will fit on the smoker rack at one time.

How Long? Until an instant-read thermometer inserted into the thickest part of the thigh near the hip joint registers 170°F, 40 minutes on the stovetop and from 30 to 60 minutes in the oven, depending on the size of the chicken(s).

Which Wood? 2½ tablespoons cherry or oak or 1½ tablespoons hickory wood chips.

Trim any excess skin from the neck end of the chicken and pull out the giblets and any pockets of fat from the cavity.

Season the chicken(s), preferably by brining them (see page 11) for 1½ hours per pound (minimum 3 hours). Alternatively, rub a generous amount of kosher salt and freshly ground black pepper into the inside and outside of each bird. If you like, stuff each chicken, brined or not, with a few whole cloves of garlic and/or a few lemon wedges.

Start the chicken(s) breast side up on the smoker rack with the smoker on the stovetop. Instead of the smoker cover, tent the smoker with heavy-duty aluminum foil (see page 5). Smoke 40 minutes.

Combo-Cooking: After the chicken(s) have been smoking 30 minutes, set the oven rack in the center position and preheat the oven to 425°F. When the chicken(s) are done smoking, remove the aluminum foil and roast the chicken in the oven until done as described above, 30 to 60 minutes, depending on the size and quanity of chicken.

Serve hot—after they've rested for 5 to 10 minutes—or at room temperature. Accompany hot smoked chicken with sautéed spinach and mashed potatoes seasoned with nutmeg and ground white pepper. Room temperature smoked chicken is delicious with a side salad of mesclun and crumbled blue cheese.

Use leftover chicken in:

Deli-Style Chicken Salad (page 120)

Baked Macaroni and Cheese with Smoked Chicken (page 123)

Smoked Chicken, String Bean, and Cauliflower Casserole (page 121)

Shredded Chicken with Peanut Sauce (page 48)

Chicken Breasts, Boneless (With or Without Skin)

When it comes to serving smoked chicken as a main course, most people will offer boneless breasts for the centerpiece of a meal and use smoked thighs as an ingredient in soups, salads, and casseroles, like the ones described later on in this chapter. I'm an exception to that rule, choosing legs over breasts for just about any chicken dish I'm preparing. Legs and thighs have more flavor and are easier to keep juicy, although with a stovetop smoker, keeping the breasts juicy is less of a problem.

How Many? Up to four 8-ounce or six 6-ounce boneless breasts will fit on the smoker rack at one time.

How Long? Until an instant-read thermometer inserted into the thickest part of the breast registers 170°F; 18 to 22 minutes for 6-ounce/¾-inch thick breasts; 22 to 25 minutes for 7-ounce/1-inch thick breasts; 25 to 30 minutes for 8-ounce/1¼-inch thick breasts.

Which Wood? Boneless chicken breasts absorb a lot of flavor and match well with a wide variety of wood. Choose 1½ tablespoons of more assertive wood chips like hickory or mesquite or 2 to 2½ tablespoons of milder wood chips like alder or cherry.

Trim any fat from the breasts before seasoning them. If you're leaving the skin on in preparation for serving the crispy-skinned variation, trim any overhanging skin and smooth the skin into an even layer over the chicken. If not, remove the skin before smoking the chicken.

Season the chicken breasts with ½ teaspoon kosher salt and a scant ⅛ teaspoon freshly ground pepper each, adjusting that amount to your taste. Or rub a generous amount of any of the rubs on pages 25–29 into both sides of the chicken. Recipes in this and other chapters that use smoked chicken as an ingredient may advise you to season the chicken differently.

Check the chicken breasts for doneness with an instant-read thermometer about 4 minutes before the end of the time outlined above.

Combo-Cooking: For crispy-skinned chicken breasts, choose a nonstick pan large enough to hold the number of chicken breasts you're serving. Heat it over medium-high heat a few minutes before the chicken breasts are done smoking.

Lift the chicken with tongs from the smoker and lay them skin side down in the pan. Cook until the skin is crispy and deep golden brown, about 3 minutes. Serve immediately.

Serve smoked chicken breasts with scalloped potatoes, a nice crisp salad, and/or simple green vegetables like buttered broccoli or sautéed spinach. They also make delicious sandwiches when paired with sliced fresh mozzarella and roasted red peppers, or with Cheddar cheese, cucumber, and honey mustard.

Use in any of these dishes:

Smoked Chicken, Pecan, and Gruyère Salad (page 74)

Smoked Turkey Hash (in place of the turkey; page 125)

Smoked Chicken and Black Bean Quesadillas (page 46)

Shredded Chicken with Peanut Sauce (page 48)

NOTE: Four 7-ounce chicken breasts will yield about 3 cups shredded cooked meat.

Chicken Thighs

How Many? Up to 6 fryer chicken thighs (about 2½ pounds) will fit on the smoker rack at one time.

How Long? Until an instant-read thermometer inserted into the thickest part of the thigh near the bone registers 170°F; 25 to 30 minutes after closing the smoker lid.

Which Wood? The richer flavor of chicken thighs benefit from more flavorful woods like hickory, corncob, or mesquite; use about 2 tablespoons of any of the above per batch.

Trim off all the skin and cut away any excess fat from the thighs before seasoning them (See Combo-Cooking under **Chicken Breasts**, page 94 if you'd like to smoke the thighs with skin on and crisp them in a pan after smoking.)

Season each chicken thigh with ½ teaspoon kosher salt and ¼ teaspoon freshly ground black pepper.

Check the thighs for doneness with an instant-read thermometer about 15 minutes into the cooking time.

Serve right out of the smoker with any of the salsas on pages 21–23 and your favorite coleslaw or any of the variations listed on page 90.

Use in the following dishes:

Smoked Chicken, Pecan, and Gruyère Salad (page 74)

Baked Macaroni and Cheese with Smoked Chicken (page 123)

Smoked Chicken, String Bean, and Cauliflower Casserole (page 121)

NOTE: Six chicken thighs will yield about 3 cups shredded cooked meat.

Chicken Wings

How Many? Up to about 1½ pounds chicken wings—which will yield about 16 pieces when trimmed as noted here—will fit on the smoker rack at one time.

How Long? Until an instant-read thermometer inserted into the thickest part of the wings registers 170°F; 20 to 25 minutes from the time the smoker top is closed.

Which Wood? Chicken wings can take more assertive woods, like 2 tablespoons of hickory or mesquite, but also work well with mellower choices like 2 tablespoons of alder or cherry.

Trim whole chicken wings into sections as described here.

Season 1½ pounds of chicken wings with 1½ teaspoons kosher salt and a generous ¼ teaspoon freshly ground black pepper.

Check the wings for doneness with an instant-read thermometer after 20 minutes.

Serve with **Smoky-Spicy Salsa** (page 21) or your favorite bottled salsa for dipping, or borrow a simple serving idea from the folks in Buffalo: after closing the lid of the smoker, slice about 1½ tablespoons butter into a heatproof mixing bowl. Set the bowl on top of the smoker to melt the butter as the wings smoke. When the wings are done, toss them in the butter, seasoning them with as much of your favorite hot red pepper sauce as you like. That, and a lot of napkins, is all you need; skip the blue cheese–celery thing.

Pass any of the sauces suggested for baby back ribs (see pages 167–168) for dipping. Or go one step beyond and glaze the wings: smoke the chicken wings. (This can be done up to two days in advance.) Heat the oven to 425°F. Line a baking

I cut wings into two parts—à la Buffalo wings—before smoking them. They absorb more flavor, are easier to smoke, and more fun to eat. If starting with whole wings, first cut off and discard the wing tips—we won't be smoking those since they have no meat. Next, cut the remaining part of the wing into two pieces at the joint. To make this easier, make a small cut near the joint and, with your hands, bend the wing until it is nearly straight. If you take a careful look at the joint, you will notice a space between the joint—that's where you want to cut. Once you do a few of these, you'll get the hang of it.

sheet with aluminum foil and spray the foil with vegetable cooking spray. Toss the wings with enough of either of the sauces to coat them lightly but thoroughly. Roast until the wings are heated through and the sauce is lightly browned, about 10 minutes.

Cornish Game Hens

How Many? Up to two 1 to 1¼-pound hens or poussins will fit on the smoker rack at one time.

How Long? Until an instant-read thermometer inserted into the thickest part of the thigh near the hip joint registers 170°F; 30 minutes on the stovetop and about 30 minutes in the oven.

Which Wood? 2 tablespoons alder, cherry, or corncob, or 1½ tablespoons hickory.

Trim any excess skin from the neck end of the hens and pull out the giblets and any pockets of fat from the cavity.

Season the hens, preferably by brining them (see page 11) for 3 hours. Or rub a generous amount of salt and pepper into the inside and outside of each bird. If you like, stuff each hen with a few whole cloves of garlic, two lemon wedges, and sprigs of whatever fresh herbs you have on hand.

Start the hens breast side up on the smoker rack with the smoker on the stovetop. Instead of the smoker cover, tent the smoker with heavy-duty aluminum foil (see page 5). Smoke 30 minutes.

Combo-Cooking: While the hens are smoking, set the rack in the center position and preheat the oven to 425°F. Stir 2 tablespoons melted butter or olive oil, ½ teaspoon kosher salt, and ¼ teaspoon freshly ground black pepper together in a small bowl. Omit the salt if you've brined the birds. When the hens are done smoking, remove the aluminum foil and brush them with the seasoned butter. Roast until done as described above, about 30 minutes, brushing once or twice with the seasoned butter.

Check the hens for doneness with an instant-read thermometer after they've been in the oven 20 minutes.

My supermarket carries fresh, free range Cornish game hens and, occasionally, poussin—baby chicken—which can be smoked according to the guidelines here. Both of these birds are just as versatile as chickens, and whole smaller birds like these make a nice change from chicken parts.

Serve the hens with fluffy mashed potatoes and sautéed spinach or, in warmer weather, with the **Shredded Duck, Toasted Hazelnut, and Watercress Salad** (page 76)—minus the duck, of course.

Whole Turkey

How Many? A whole 10-pound or smaller turkey will fit on the smoker rack.

How Long? Until an instant-read thermometer inserted into the thickest part of the thigh next to the bone registers 170°F; for a 10-pound turkey, 45 minutes on the stovetop plus 1½ to 2 hours in the oven.

Which Wood? Like all poultry, the mellower flavors of woods like alder, cherry, and apple work well with turkey, but the bird's size means it can take more assertive woods like corncob or hickory, if you prefer.

Trim any excess skin from the neck cavity and pull any solid fat from inside the body cavity.

Season the turkey, preferably by brining (see page 11) for 10 to 14 hours. Or rub a generous amount of salt and pepper into the inside and outside of the turkey and refrigerate for 2 to 4 hours.

Start the turkey breast side up on the smoker rack with the smoker on the stovetop. Instead of the smoker cover, tent the smoker with heavy-duty aluminum foil (see page 5). Start with the heat on medium, then reduce the heat slightly. Smoke 45 minutes.

Combo-Cooking: After the turkey has been smoking 20 minutes, set the oven rack in the lower third of the oven and preheat the oven to 400°F. When the turkey is done

BUTTER UP!

When smoking a whole turkey, chicken, or cornish hen, try this simple flavor booster, whether or not you've brined the bird. Before smoking, mix 3 tablespoons finely chopped fresh herbs—a mix of sage, thyme, and savory is nice—together with 4 tablespoons softened butter. Starting at the neck, wiggle a couple of fingers underneath the skin to separate it from the meat. Work your way carefully over the breast and thighs, gently separating the skin from meat to avoid tearing the skin. Next, smear the butter over the meat but below the skin, then pat the skin back into place.

smoking, lift one corner of the aluminum foil to allow steam to escape, then remove the foil and set the whole smoker on the oven rack. Roast until an instant-read thermometer inserted into the thickest part of the thigh next to the bone registers 170°F, about 1 hour and 45 minutes for a 10-pound turkey.

Check the turkey for doneness with an instant-read thermometer after the turkey has been roasting 1½ hours.

Serve with your favorite turkey trimmings and discover how different they taste next to a smoked turkey. The **Brown Gravy** (page 20) and **Cranberry Relish** (page 24) are two good starting choices.

Turkey Breast

How Many? Up to an 8-pound bone-in turkey breast will fit on the smoker rack.

How Long? Until an instant-read thermometer inserted into the thickest part of the breast near the bone registers 170°F; 40 minutes on the stovetop and about 45 minutes in the oven (for a 5-pound turkey breast).

Which Wood? 2 to 3 tablespoons hickory, alder, apple, or oak wood chips.

Season the turkey breast, preferably by brining (see page 11), about 1½ hours per pound or, alternatively by rubbing a generous amount of salt and pepper directly onto the meat. Do this by gently working your hand between the skin and meat, loosening the skin as you go and being careful not to tear the skin.

Start smoking the turkey skin side up on the smoker rack with the smoker on the stovetop. Instead of the smoker cover, tent the smoker with heavy-duty aluminum foil (see page 5). Smoke for 40 minutes.

Combo-Cooking: After the turkey has been smoking 30 minutes, place the rack in the center position and preheat the oven to 425°F. When the turkey is done smoking, uncover the smoker and roast until done as described above, about 45 minutes.

Check the turkey after it has been in the oven 40 minutes (for a 5-pound breast) or about 1 hour (for an 8-pound breast).

Serve the turkey hot, after it has rested 10 to 15 minutes, or at room temperature. Chilled leftover smoked turkey breast makes excellent sandwiches. I like them with mayonnaise on one slice of bread and the **Cranberry Relish** (page 24) on the other slice.

Use leftover smoked turkey in:

Turkey-Mushroom-Barley Soup (page 68)

Deli-Style Chicken (or Turkey) Salad (page 120)

Smoked Turkey Hash (page 125)

Turkey Thighs

How Many? Up to four 1 to 1¼-pound or two 2-pound turkey thighs will fit on the smoker rack at one time.

How Long? Until an instant-read thermometer inserted into the thickest part of the thigh registers 170°F; about 45 minutes after closing the smoker lid for 1¼-pound thighs. If your turkey thighs haven't reached 170°F in 45 minutes, see Combo-Cooking.

Which Wood? 3 tablespoons mesquite or hickory wood chips.

Trim off the skin by tugging it off and cut away any excess fat.

Season the thighs by rubbing ¾ teaspoon kosher salt and ¼ teaspoon freshly ground black pepper into each. Or brine them (see page 11).

Combo-Cooking: If the thighs aren't ready after 45 minutes of smoking, heat the oven to 400°F and roast the thighs in the smoker without the lid until an instant-read thermometer inserted into the thickest part of the thigh registers 170°F.

Check 1¼-pound thighs for doneness after 45 minutes of smoking.

Serve turkey thighs hot out of the smoker with **Brown Gravy** (page 20) and a side of mashed potatoes.

Use them in:

Turkey-Mushroom-Barley Soup (page 68)

Smoked Turkey Hash (page 125)

NOTE: Two 1¼-pound turkey thighs will yield about 3½ cups diced smoked turkey meat.

When it comes to value and flavor, it's hard to beat smoked turkey thighs. If the turkey thighs are your main course, and they are larger than 1¼ pounds each, I suggest brining them before you smoke them. If they are going into other dishes like salads or soups, brining isn't as important. Once shredded or diced, they'll pick up seasoning from whatever dish they're in.

Turkey Wings

I don't smoke turkey wings to eat on their own because they can be a little tough—as in doggie-chew-toy tough. But they add tremendous flavor to soups, stews, and, believe it or not, a pot of tomato sauce destined for a big platter of pasta. Depending on where you shop, you will find either whole (three segment) turkey wings or wings that have been cut into individual segments at the joint. Go with the wings already cut into segments whenever possible—the whole ones can be a bear to cut up. And try to pick whole wings that are no heavier than 1¼ pounds each. They will fit into the smoker nicely and will cook more evenly.

How Many? Up to 3 whole small wings (about 1¼ pounds each) or 6 wing segments from smaller wings (about 4 pounds) will fit on the smoker rack at one time.

How Long? Until an instant-read thermometer inserted into the thickest part of the wing near the bone registers 170°F; about 45 minutes after closing the smoker lid. (To be sure, probe a few different pieces before deciding they're done.)

Which Wood? 1½ tablespoons hickory or mesquite wood chips or 2 tablespoons alder or cherry wood chips.

Trim any excess fat from the wings and cut the wings into individual segments if necessary: first cut off and discard the wing tips—we won't be smoking those since they have no meat. Next, cut the remaining part of the wing into two pieces at the joint. To make this easier, make a small cut near the joint and, with your hands, bend the wing until it is nearly straight. If you take a careful look at the joint, you will notice a space between the joint—that's where you want to cut. Once you do a few of these, you'll get the hang of where to cut.

Season each wing section with ½ teaspoon kosher salt and a scant ¼ teaspoon freshly ground black pepper. Rub the seasoning vigorously into the turkey.

Combo-Cooking may be necessary with larger wings. If the turkey wings haven't reached the proper temperature after 45 minutes, heat the oven to 350°F and bake the wings until done as described above.

Check the wings for doneness with an instant-read thermometer after 35 minutes.

Use smoked turkey wings to season your favorite bean soups, vegetable soups, baked bean dishes, or in one of these dishes:

Split Pea and Smoked Turkey Soup (page 70)

Rigatoni with Smoked Turkey and Hot Cherry Peppers (page 126)

Whole Duck

Smoke-roasting a duck delivers the best of two worlds: crispy, browned skin and juicy, rich-tasting meat. If two of you are sharing the duck, you might want to

The simplest way to carve and serve a duck: cut through the skin between the breast and thigh, following the curve of the thigh. Bend the leg away from the body until you can see where the hip joint connects to the backbone. Remove the leg by cutting along the backbone, wiggling the knife to separate the thigh bone from the hip bone. You may serve the leg whole or cut into two pieces through the knee joint. Secondly, cut thin slices from the breasts, holding the knife parallel to the breastbone. To get the most from the duck breast, let the knife follow the gentle curve of the breastbone as you carve.

How Many? One 5 to 6-pound duck will fit on the smoker rack.

How Long? Until an instant-read thermometer registers 160°F when inserted into the joint where the thigh meets the backbone; 30 minutes on the stovetop and 30 to 35 minutes in a 425°F oven.

Which Wood? 2 tablespoons of fruit wood chips like cherry or apple. Avoid woods with a twang, like pecan, corncob, or mesquite.

Trim the excess fat and skin from around the neck cavity. Pull out the neck, giblets, and any pockets of fat from the body cavity. Rinse the cavities and pat them dry with paper towels. Score the skin over the breast and thighs with a very sharp knife or a razor just deep enough to cut through the skin and into the fat. Don't cut into the meat.

Season the inside of the duck generously with salt and pepper and rub salt and pepper into the skin as well.

Start the duck breast side up on the smoker rack. Tent the smoker with heavy-duty aluminum foil (see page 5) and smoke 30 minutes.

Combo-Cooking: While the duck is smoking, place the rack in the center position and preheat the oven to 425°F. After the duck is done smoking, remove the aluminum foil cover and roast until done as described above.

Check the duck for doneness with an instant-read thermometer after it has been in the oven 25 minutes.

Serve the duck after it has rested 10 minutes.

Leftover duck can be used instead of turkey in:

Smoked Turkey Hash (page 125) or in

Shredded Duck, Toasted Hazelnut, and Watercress Salad (page 76)

carve the breasts for one meal, then prepare the legs like the Deviled Chicken Thighs on page 115 for a second meal.

Duck Breasts

If you can find boneless duck breasts—some supermarkets now sell them—you will have the basis for many dishes, including the recipes at the end of this chapter. The legs, smoked separately, yield their own group of delicious dishes. Usually, smoking is all the cooking most foods need; but some ingredients benefit immeasurably from additional cooking after smoking. Duck breasts definitely fall into the second camp. Lightly smoked duck breasts, finished in a hot skillet to crisp the skin but leave the meat rosy, are one of the best reasons for using a smoker.

How Many? Up to four 8-ounce boneless duck breasts will fit on the smoker rack at one time.

How Long? Until an instant-read thermometer inserted into the thickest part of the breast registers 140°F, about 20 minutes in the smoker and 5 minutes in a skillet to crisp the skin and finish the cooking.

Which Wood? Choose 1½ tablespoons of any fruit wood chips like apple or cherry, or an equal amount of pecan wood chips for a little bite. Or, take a page from classical Chinese cooking and use 2 tablespoons of fragrant loose tea, like jasmine, in place of the wood chips.

Trim the duck breast by laying it skin side down on the cutting board and cutting off any overhanging skin and fat. Check, too, for small pieces of bone. Turn the duck skin side up and, with a small sharp knife, score the skin at 1-inch intervals, cutting only about halfway through the fat, not all the way through to the breast meat.

Season each breast with ½ teaspoon kosher salt and a scant ¼ teaspoon freshly ground black pepper, rubbing the seasoning well into the meat and skin sides of the breasts.

Start the breasts skin side up and smoke 20 minutes.

Combo-Cooking: Crisp up the skin and finish cooking the duck breasts by laying them skin side down in a preheated heavy cast iron or nonstick pan over medium-low heat. Cook until the skin is well-browned and crisp, about 5 minutes.

Check the duck breasts for doneness with an instant-read thermometer after 4 minutes in the pan; they are ready when an instant-read thermometer inserted into the thickest part of the breast registers 140°F.

The duck breasts can be smoked up to one day in advance and refrigerated until needed. Start refrigerated smoked duck breasts in a cold pan and cook until crispy and 140°F at the thickest part, about 10 minutes.

Serve smoked duck breasts with mashed parsnips and potatoes (roughly equal parts of each), glazed turnips, or sautéed Swiss chard, or use them in the following dishes:

Tea-Smoked Duck with Asian Slaw (page 128)

Shredded Duck, Toasted Hazelnut, and Watercress Salad (page 76)

Duck Legs

If you've mastered the art of breaking down a duck into boneless breasts and bone-in legs, or if your market sells duck legs, use them here. You'll be rewarded with pleasantly chewy, mildly smoky duck that is good on its own or in a salad. I like to leave the skin on my duck legs, crisp them up as described under Combo-Cooking, and serve them with a little grainy mustard.

How Many? Up to 4 whole duck legs (about 3½ pounds) will fit on the smoker rack at one time.

How Long? Until an instant-read thermometer inserted into the thickest part of the thigh next to the bone registers 170°F; 35 to 40 minutes from the time the smoker lid is closed.

Which Wood? 4 to 5 teaspoons oak, apple, or corncob wood chips bring out the sweet taste of duck. I stay away from stronger woods with duck.

Trim all the skin (by simply pulling it off) and excess fat from the duck legs if you like before seasoning and smoking them; if you leave the skin on, Combo-Cooking will explain how to crisp it up.

Season each leg with ¾ teaspoon kosher salt and a scant ¼ teaspoon freshly ground black pepper, rubbing the seasoning well into the meat.

Check the legs for doneness with an instant-read thermometer after 35 minutes.

Combo-Cooking: For crispy-skinned duck legs, smoke the legs with the skins on for 30 minutes. Preheat the oven to 400°F while the duck legs are smoking. When the duck legs are done smoking, remove the lid and roast until the skin is golden brown and crisp, about 15 minutes.

Serve smoked duck legs with a soft and creamy polenta, or use them to prepare:

Deviled Chicken Thighs (in place of the chicken; page 115)

Shredded Duck, Toasted Hazelnut, and Watercress Salad (page 76)

Honey-Lemon Chicken Breasts

Four 7-ounce smoked
boneless chicken breasts,
with or without skin

¼ cup honey

½ lemon, sliced very thin

1 teaspoon kosher salt

½ teaspoon freshly ground
black pepper

2 tablespoons apple, cherry,
or hickory wood chips

Tangy-sweet, smoke-edged, and, best of all, almost effortless, these chicken breasts are delicious on their own, or in salads and sandwiches. If you like your chicken breasts with the skin on (see page 94), work a little of the marinade under the skin with your fingers.

MAKES 4 SERVINGS

1. Trim any excess fat or cartilage from the chicken breasts.

2. Bring the honey and lemon slices to a boil in a small saucepan over medium-low heat. Adjust the heat so the honey is boiling gently and cook until the glaze is thick and syrupy and reduced by about half. (At first, as the juice is drawn from the lemon slices, the marinade with thin out. It will thicken as it cooks.) Remove from the heat and stir in the salt and pepper.

3. Pour all but a tablespoon or two of the glaze into a shallow bowl. Turn the chicken breasts in the glaze to coat them all evenly. Marinate the chicken for 30 minutes at room temperature, or up to 8 hours in the refrigerator.

4. Set up the smoker using the wood chips and smoke the chicken breasts according to the directions on page 94. Choose the Combo-Cooking option if using skin-on chicken breasts. Serve warm, brushed with the remaining glaze.

Herby Chicken Breasts with Pipérade

Pipérade is a mix of onions and peppers cooked slowly to bring out their sweetness. I cook my pipérade until the peppers "melt" and turn super sweet, but you might prefer to cook yours about half as long, leaving them slightly crisp. Taste along the way and stop when you're happy. I prefer skinless chicken breasts for this recipe. If you'd like to leave the skins on, follow the directions for Combo-Cooking on page 94.

MAKES 4 SERVINGS

FOR THE PIPÉRADE

3 tablespoons extra virgin olive oil

½ cup diced (¼-inch) smoked ham

2 large yellow onions, sliced ½ inch

Kosher salt

Freshly ground black pepper

2 red bell peppers, cores, seeds, and membranes removed, cut into ¼-inch strips

2 yellow bell peppers, cores, seeds, and membranes removed, cut into ¼-inch strips

FOR THE CHICKEN

Four 7-ounce smoked chicken breasts

1 tablespoon Mushroom-Herb Rub (page 27)

1½ tablespoons apple, cherry, or alder wood chips

1. Make the pipérade. Heat the oil in a large, heavy skillet over medium heat. Add the ham and cook, stirring occasionally, until lightly browned, about 4 minutes. Stir in the onions, season lightly with salt and pepper, and cook until softened and lightly browned, about 8 minutes. Stir in the red and yellow peppers and season them lightly with salt. Adjust the heat to medium-low and cook, stirring often, until they are very tender and sweet, about 30 minutes. The pipérade can be made several hours in advance and reheated over low heat.

2. To smoke the chicken, pat the chicken breasts dry with paper towels. Massage the herb rub into both sides of the breasts, dividing the rub evenly. Set up the smoker using the wood chips and smoke the chicken breasts according to the directions on page 94.

3. Reheat the pipérade if necessary. Serve the chicken nestled into a bed of the pipérade.

Deviled Chicken Thighs

8 skinless smoked chicken
    thighs

2 cups day-old, dense-
    textured bread cubes

Vegetable cooking spray

¼ cup Dijon mustard

3 tablespoons melted unsalted
    butter

1 tablespoon dry white wine or
    water

1 teaspoon dried thyme

You can use store-bought breadcrumbs to coat these smoky-spicy chicken thighs, but homemade, coarse-textured crumbs are a lot more fun. Or, seek out panko, Japanese-style breadcrumbs, which are available in some specialty food stores and supermarkets. The bread used to make the crumbs should be day-old, but not stale. Completely dry bread yields very fine crumbs.

MAKES 4 SERVINGS

1. Smoke the chicken thighs according to the directions on page 96 and cool them to room temperature. The chicken may be smoked up to two days in advance. Cover with plastic wrap and store in the refrigerator.

2. Place the bread cubes in a food processor fitted with the metal blade. Process to very coarse crumbs. Spread the crumbs out on a baking sheet and let them dry for about an hour.

3. Preheat the oven to 400°F. Spray a baking sheet with vegetable cooking spray (not necessary if you are using a non-stick baking sheet).

4. Stir the mustard, butter, wine, and thyme together in a small bowl until blended. Brush the meaty side of the chicken thighs generously with the mustard mixture, then pat on a thick, even layer of breadcrumbs. Arrange the thighs crumb side up on the prepared baking sheet.

5. Bake until the chicken is heated through and the crumb coating is deep golden brown and crispy, about 20 minutes. Serve hot or at room temperature.

Chicken and Yellow Rice

MAKES 4 SERVINGS

8 skinless smoked chicken thighs or 16 pieces smoked chicken wings

3 tablespoons olive oil

1 large Spanish onion, diced (about 1⅔ cups)

3 garlic cloves, thinly sliced

1 cup pimiento-stuffed olives, drained and coarsely chopped

½ teaspoon turmeric

4 cups homemade or canned reduced-sodium chicken broth

2 cups long-grain rice

⅓ cup toasted sliced almonds

1. Smoke the chicken pieces according to the directions on page 96 or 97. Cool them to room temperature.

2. Heat the olive oil in a 6-quart Dutch oven or heavy pot over medium heat. Stir in the onion and garlic and cook, stirring, until the onion is golden brown, about 10 minutes. Stir in the olives, turmeric, and smoked chicken pieces.

3. Pour in the broth and bring to a boil. Stir in the rice, then wiggle the pot so the ingredients are covered by the broth and settle into a more or less even layer. Adjust the heat so the liquid is at a gentle boil. Boil until the liquid barely covers the rice.

4. Give the rice and chicken a big, gentle mixing. Adjust the heat so the liquid is barely simmering. Re-cover the pot and continue cooking until the rice is tender and the liquid is absorbed, about 20 minutes. Remove from the heat and let stand uncovered 5 minutes.

5. Sprinkle the almonds over the rice and serve directly from the casserole, or pile the chicken and rice on a platter and scatter the almonds over the top.

Jamaican Jerk Chicken

2½ pounds chicken thighs, with or without skin

¼ cup lime juice, preferably fresh-squeezed

1½ teaspoons kosher salt

FOR THE MARINADE

1 medium yellow onion, coarsely chopped (about 1½ cups)

6 scallions, trimmed and coarsely chopped (about 1 cup)

Chiles, stemmed and coarsely chopped (see Note)

2 tablespoons soy sauce

2 tablespoons light or dark brown sugar

4 garlic cloves

Six ¼-inch slices peeled fresh ginger

2 teaspoons dried thyme

1 teaspoon ground allspice

½ teaspoon grated nutmeg

3 tablespoons hickory or mesquite wood chips

1. Place the chicken thighs in a heavy-duty resealable plastic bag. Stir the lime juice and salt together in a small bowl until the salt is dissolved, then pour the mixture into the bag. Squeeze out most of the air in the bag, seal the bag, and refrigerate 2 hours, turning the bag two or three times.

2. Process all the marinade ingredients in a food processor fitted with the metal blade or in a blender until the mixture is fairly smooth. Scrape the marinade into the bag with the chicken, seal the bag securely, and mush it around to coat the chicken with marinade. Marinate at least one day or up to two days. (Marinate chicken wings a maximum of one day; seafood steaks 6 hours, and shrimp 3 hours.)

A look at the roster of ingredients that go into this marinade gives you an idea of the cross-cultural nature of jerk, Jamaica's national culinary treasure. The recipe below is for chicken thighs, but you could use the marinade for 2½ pounds of chicken wings as well. (See page 97 for instructions on cutting them into pieces.) You can also marinate shelled shrimp or thick, sturdy cuts of fish like mako shark or swordfish steaks, or salmon or mahi-mahi fillets. Marinate seafood for 6 hours at most (or 3 hours in the case of shrimp) and skip the final baking described here.

I prefer my chicken without skin on this one—the wet, chunky marinade clings better to skinless chicken pieces. The first time you smoke a batch of jerk, try a few pieces each way, and make up your mind. Chilled, this makes an excellent dish to bring on a picnic.

MAKES ABOUT 1½ CUPS, enough to marinate 2½ pounds of poultry or fish

3. Empty the bag of chicken into a colander and drain briefly. Transfer the pieces onto the smoker rack, smoothing off all but a thin, even layer of the marinade as you go. Using the wood chips, set up the smoker and smoke the chicken according to the directions on page 96 for 30 minutes. After the chicken has been smoking 20 minutes, preheat the oven to 400°F.

4. After the chicken is done smoking, remove the lid and roast until well browned, about 20 minutes. Cool the chicken at least 10 minutes before serving. Serve hot, room temperature, or cold.

NOTE: You can go in any direction with the chiles, depending on your preference and what is available. If you like things fairly spicy, use 4 to 8 Scotch bonnet or habanero chiles or 6 jalapeños. Tone it down or jack it up from there, as you see fit.

SMOKIN' EXTRAS
Lemonade

To get the most juice out of a lemon, start with room temperature lemons. Roll the lemons on a hard surface under the palm of your hands until you feel them soften. Then go ahead and juice them as you normally do.

Prepare a simple syrup by stirring equal amounts of sugar and water together in a heavy saucepan over medium heat until the sugar is dissolved. Cool the syrup to room temperature and pour it into a jar with a tight fitting lid. Store at room temperature until needed.

To make lemonade, pour cool water into a pitcher. Add fresh-squeezed lemon juice until the mixture is as tart as you like. Pour in as much of the simple syrup as you like. Adjust with more lemon juice if you like, then pour over ice in a tall glass.

When it comes to drinks with smoked foods, especially spicy smoked foods like the preceding Jerk Chicken, it's hard to beat lemonade. Here is a simple way to prepare it. In lemonade season, prepare the syrup described here and keep it at room temperature.

Deli-Style Chicken (or Turkey) Salad

In all its simplicity, this reminds me of the lobster rolls you can buy everywhere in Maine—chunks of lobster, some celery, and mayonnaise—served on a squishy-soft hot dog roll. (Not a bad way to serve this, by the way.) The trick is to thin out the mayonnaise a bit so it penetrates the chunks of chicken or turkey. You can gussy this up with toasted sliced almonds folded in at the last minute, or with diced dill pickle. Serve the salad as is on crackers, or fold in some halved, juicy cherry tomatoes and spoon it over greens. It's best, in my opinion, sandwiched between slices of pumpernickel bread with a few crispy slices of bacon to keep it company.

MAKES 2 SERVINGS

⅓ cup Hellman's or other mayonnaise

2 cups diced (about ¾-inch) smoked chicken or turkey

2 large celery stalks, diced (about ¾ cup)

Kosher salt

Freshly ground black pepper

Stir the mayonnaise and 2 tablespoons water together in a mixing bowl. Stir in the chicken and celery and season the salad lightly with salt (if necessary) and generously with pepper. Let stand until the chicken has absorbed some of the dressing, about 30 minutes at room temperature or up to a day in the refrigerator. Check the seasoning and bring the salad to room temperature, if necessary, before serving.

Smoked Chicken, String Bean, and Cauliflower Casserole

1 pound sturdy (not too thin) string beans, trimmed and cut in half crosswise

½ head cauliflower, center stem removed and cut into florets the size of your thumb (about 4 cups)

3 tablespoons unsalted butter

4 garlic cloves, chopped fine

4 tablespoons all-purpose flour

3 cups hot homemade or canned reduced-sodium chicken broth

½ cup milk

1½ cups shredded smoked chicken

6 scallions, trimmed and thinly sliced

Kosher salt

Freshly ground black pepper

⅓ cup grated Parmesan cheese or the breadcrumb topping from Baked Macaroni and Cheese with Smoked Chicken (page 123)

I borrowed this idea from Southern cooks who treat their string beans to a long slow cooking with smoked ham hocks. The beans absorb the flavor of the ham and develop a richer taste of their own. Smoked chicken works the same magic in this casserole, which you can prepare up to a day in advance.

This is dinner for me— but serve it with steamed rice or take-out vegetable stir-fried rice if you like. Or toast thick slices of country bread until crispy and lay them in the bottom of a warm soup bowl, then spoon the casserole over it. Now you're talking.

MAKES 4 SERVINGS

1. Bring a large pot of salted water to a boil. Stir in the string beans and cook for 4 minutes. Stir in the cauliflower and cook until both vegetables are barely tender, about 4 minutes. Drain the vegetables in a colander, spread them out in an even layer in an 11-inch oval baking dish (or any 6-cup baking dish that is about 1½-inches deep). Let them stand while you put together the rest of the recipe.

2. Preheat the oven to 375°F. Heat the butter in a medium saucepan over medium heat until foaming. Stir in the garlic and cook, stirring once or twice until light golden brown, about 2 minutes. Stir in the flour and stir constantly for 3 minutes. Switch over to a whisk and slowly pour in the broth, whisking constantly. Whisk in the milk and bring to a simmer, whisking constantly. Simmer 5 minutes, whisking occasionally, and remove from the heat. Stir in the smoked

chicken, scallions, and salt and pepper to taste. Spoon the sauce over the vegetables in the baking dish. You can bake the casserole now or refrigerate it for up to one day.

3. Cover the top of the casserole with an even layer of the Parmesan. Bake until the juices are bubbling and the top is golden brown, about 50 minutes (a few minutes longer for a refrigerated casserole). Let stand 5 minutes before serving.

Baked Macaroni and Cheese with Smoked Chicken

3 cups elbow pasta

FOR THE BREADCRUMB TOPPING (or use plain breadcrumbs)

¼ cup breadcrumbs

¼ cup grated Parmesan cheese

2 tablespoons unsalted butter, melted

4 tablespoons unsalted butter

¼ cup all-purpose flour

3 cups milk, at room temperature

Large pinch grated nutmeg

Kosher salt

Freshly ground black pepper

1½ cups coarsely shredded Jarlsberg cheese

1½ cups coarsely shredded mild to medium Cheddar

1½ cups shredded smoked chicken

1 cup frozen peas, defrosted

3 tablespoons chopped fresh flat-leaf parsley, optional

I chose the cheeses listed here to give the casserole a mild, mellow flavor that won't overpower the smoked chicken. If you like, switch to a sharper Cheddar or replace the Jarlsberg altogether with Cheddar.

MAKES 4 SERVINGS

1. Bring a large saucepan of salted water to a boil. Stir in the pasta and cook, stirring often until the pasta is al dente, about 8 minutes. (It should be very firm to the bite; it will cook more in the oven.)

2. While the pasta is cooking, preheat the oven to 375°F. Stir the breadcrumbs, grated Parmesan, and 2 tablespoons melted butter together in a small bowl. Set the topping aside.

3. Drain the pasta in a colander and run it under cold water, bouncing it around gently, until it is cool to the touch. Let it drain in the sink while you put the rest of the recipe together.

4. Dry out the pasta cooking pot, set it over medium heat, and add 4 tablespoons butter. When it is bubbling, whisk in the flour. Continue cooking, whisking constantly, 3

minutes. Pour in the milk slowly, whisking constantly. Bring to a boil, then adjust the heat so the sauce is simmering. Add the nutmeg and salt and pepper to taste. Cook 5 minutes, whisking often. Pay close attention to the sides and bottom of the pot, where the sauce will stick and burn if you let it.

5. Remove the sauce from the heat and stir in the shredded cheese until it is melted into the sauce. Fold in the chicken, peas, and parsley, if using. Stir in the pasta until completely coated with sauce and the chicken and peas are evenly distributed throughout. Pour or ladle the pasta into an 11-inch oval baking dish, or any other 6-cup baking dish that is about 1½ inches deep. (You can prepare the macaroni and cheese to this point up to one day in advance and store it covered with plastic wrap in the refrigerator. Let stand at room temperature one hour before baking.) Cover the top of the macaroni and cheese with an even layer of the breadcrumb topping. Bake until the sauce is bubbling and the top is golden brown, 45 to 50 minutes. Let stand 5 minutes before serving.

Smoked Turkey Hash

2 small Idaho potatoes (about
1 pound) or an equal
weight of Yukon gold
potatoes, peeled and cut
into rough ½-inch pieces

2 tablespoons vegetable oil

2 tablespoons unsalted butter

1 large yellow onion, diced
½ inch (about 2 cups)

2 medium celery stalks,
trimmed and diced
½ inch (about ½ cup)

Kosher salt

½ teaspoon dried thyme

2 cups diced (½-inch)
smoked turkey or chicken

¼ cup chopped fresh flat-leaf
parsley

Freshly ground black pepper

½ cup homemade or canned
reduced-sodium chicken
broth

You can, of course, use chicken here instead of turkey, but there always seems to be more turkey leftovers in our house. Poached or fried eggs and crispy toast are a must.

MAKES 4 SERVINGS

1. Cook the potatoes in a medium saucepan of boiling salted water for 3 minutes. Drain and set aside.

2. Heat the oil and butter in a large, heavy nonstick pan over medium heat until the butter is foaming. Stir in the onion and celery, season lightly with salt and cook, stirring, until the onion is wilted, about 4 minutes. Add the thyme and potatoes and cook, stirring fairly often, until the potatoes are barely tender and lightly browned, about 12 minutes.

3. Stir in the turkey and parsley, season the hash with salt and pepper and cook, stirring frequently, until the potatoes are tender and all the ingredients are golden brown, about 10 minutes.

4. Pour in the broth, bring to a boil and stir gently until the broth is evaporated. Press the hash with a metal spatula firmly into an even layer. Cook until the underside of the hash is crispy and well browned, about 5 minutes. Serve hot.

NOTE: If you like your hash extra crispy, flip the hash in sections—don't worry about doing it perfectly—and cook until the second side is browned.

Rigatoni with Smoked Turkey and Hot Cherry Peppers

Most recipes call for seeding canned tomatoes, but to me the real problem is the cores. They never really get tender, so you end up chomping on these hard little nubbins when you should be enjoying your pasta. You can kill two birds with one stone (i.e., get rid of seeds *and* cores) by following the directions. Good advice not only for this recipe, but when cooking with canned tomatoes in general.

This recipe will make about 6 cups of sauce. You'll need about 4 cups to dress a pound of pasta, so use the remaining for another pasta meal, or spoon it over steamed white rice or Yukon gold potatoes mashed with the skins left on.

MAKES 4 GENEROUS OR
6 LIGHTER SERVINGS,
WITH 2 CUPS
LEFTOVER SAUCE

4 smoked turkey wing sections (about 2½ pounds)

One 32-ounce can Italian plum tomatoes

¼ cup olive oil

1 large yellow onion, cut in half and sliced ¼ inch (about 2 cups)

4 garlic cloves, peeled and sliced

2 bottled hot cherry peppers, cored, seeded, and cut into thin strips

Kosher salt

2 tablespoons tomato paste

½ cup dry red wine

1 cup homemade or canned reduced-sodium chicken broth

1 pound rigatoni

¼ cup chopped fresh basil or flat-leaf parsley

Grated Parmesan cheese or Pecorino Romano

1. Smoke the turkey wings according to the directions on page 106. This can be done up to two days in advance of making the sauce. Wrap the turkey wings in plastic wrap and store them in the refrigerator until needed.

2. Drain the tomatoes in a colander over a bowl. Locate the core on the tomatoes and gently pull it out, taking as many seeds along with the cores as you can. Don't worry about any seeds you leave behind. Chop the tomatoes coarsely by hand or by squeezing them with your fingers right in the colander. Return the tomatoes to the liquid in the bowl.

3. Heat the olive oil in a 4-quart heavy pot over medium heat. Stir in the onion, garlic, and cherry peppers. Season lightly with salt and cook, stirring occasionally, until the onions are crisp-tender, about 8 minutes.

4. Stir in the tomato paste and cook, stirring once or twice, until the paste bubbles and takes on an orange tint, about 3 minutes. Pour in the wine, bring it to a boil, and cook for a minute or two.

5. Carefully pour the tomatoes, their liquid, and the chicken broth into the pot, tuck the wings into the tomatoes, and bring to a boil. Adjust the heat so the sauce is simmering and cook, covered, until the turkey meat begins to fall from the bones, about 1 hour. Pluck the wings from the sauce and set them aside to cool. Remove the sauce from the heat.

6. When the wings are cool enough to handle, pull off the skin and remove the meat from the bones, shredding it coarsely as you go. Stir the meat into the sauce. Taste and season with salt if necessary. The sauce can be prepared in advance and refrigerated for up to two days or frozen for up to two months.

7. About half an hour before you're ready to serve the pasta, heat a large pot of salted water to a boil. Bring 4 cups of the sauce to a simmer. (Refrigerate or freeze any remaining sauce.) Stir the rigatoni into the water and continue stirring gently until the water returns to a boil. Cook, stirring occasionally, until the pasta is al dente, about 10 minutes. Ladle off and reserve about a cup of the pasta cooking liquid and drain the pasta well. Return the pasta to the pot and place it over low heat. Stir in the reserved 4 cups of sauce and the basil. If the sauce doesn't flow smoothly over the pasta, stir in the reserved pasta cooking water as necessary.

8. Remove the pot from the heat, stir in a handful of grated Parmesan, and spoon the pasta onto a serving platter. Pass additional grated Parmesan at the table if you like.

NOTE: Always add grated Parmesan to pasta at the last minute and off the heat. Cooking Parmesan will separate the fat from the protein and turn the cheese stringy.

Tea-Smoked Duck with Asian Slaw

To serve this as a first course for four people, cut the quantities in half. Half a duck breast would look a little odd on a plate, though, so I suggest you slice and "fan" the duck as described in the last step of the recipe. Make sure you have a sharp carving knife handy for evenly thin slices.

FOR THE DUCK

4 smoked boneless duck breasts (about 1¾ pounds)

1½ teaspoons kosher salt

½ teaspoon freshly ground Szechwan pepper or black pepper

Finely grated zest of 1 orange

Large pinch ground cloves

FOR THE SLAW

1 small head (about 1¾ pounds) Napa cabbage, wilted outer leaves removed

2 celery stalks, trimmed and very thinly sliced (about ⅔ cup)

2 carrots, trimmed, peeled, and coarsely shredded (about ½ cup)

4 scallions, trimmed and very thinly sliced

3 tablespoons chopped fresh cilantro, optional

2 teaspoons celery seed, optional

3 tablespoons mild white wine vinegar or rice vinegar

2 tablespoons Asian sesame oil

1 tablespoon sugar

1 teaspoon kosher salt

3 tablespoons loose jasmine tea or other tea leaves

1. Trim the duck breasts and score the skin according to the directions on page 110. Stir the salt, pepper, orange zest, and cloves together in a small bowl and rub the spice mixture into the meat side of the breasts. Cover with plastic wrap and refrigerate at least 4 hours or up to one day.

2. Make the slaw about 1 hour before serving the duck: Cut the Napa cabbage in half through the core. Cut out the core from both halves and shred the cabbage fine. Toss the Napa cabbage, celery, carrots, scallions, cilantro, and celery seed, if using, together in a large bowl. Stir the vinegar, sesame oil, sugar, and 1 teaspoon salt together in a small bowl until

the sugar is dissolved. Pour the dressing over the vegetables and toss well. Let the slaw stand at room temperature, tossing it often, until the cabbage is wilted but still crunchy and the vegetables have absorbed the flavor of the dressing.

3. Set up the smoker using tea leaves instead of wood chips. Smoke and pan-crisp the duck breasts according to the directions on page 110. Let them stand at room temperature a few minutes.

4. While the duck breasts are resting, toss the slaw one last time and add salt, pepper, sesame oil, or vinegar if necessary.

5. Mound the slaw on one side of each of four plates. Serve the duck breasts whole or, if you like, slice them thinly on the bias with a thin-bladed sharp knife and fan the slices in a crescent around the slaw. The duck does not have to be piping hot. In fact, I like it better closer to room temperature.

Quail with Wild Rice Stuffing

Most quail you will find in retail markets, whether fresh or frozen, is "semi-boneless," meaning only the drumstick and wing bones are left in place. This makes them easier to eat and means the birds can hold more stuffing than a bird with all its bones. If you find bone-in birds, or hunt your own, the following recipe makes about twice as much stuffing as you'll need. Heat up the stuffing that doesn't fit in the birds and serve the quail alongside it.

MAKES 2 SERVINGS

4 semi-boneless or bone-in quail, about 4 ounces each

Kosher salt

Freshly ground black pepper

½ cup wild rice

2 tablespoons unsalted butter

2 celery stalks, trimmed and diced fine (about ⅔ cup)

½ cup diced (¼-inch) smoked ham

3 scallions, trimmed and thinly sliced (about ⅓ cup)

Cranberry juice

¼ cup dried cherries or cranberries

⅓ cup toasted walnut pieces

1½ tablespoons cherry, alder, or oak wood chips

1. Remove any giblets from inside the quails if necessary. Pat the quail dry inside and outside with paper towels and season them generously inside and out with salt and pepper. Cover the quail with plastic wrap and let stand at room temperature 30 minutes or, preferably, refrigerate at least 4 hours or up to one day.

2. Bring a medium saucepan of salted water to a boil. Stir in the wild rice and cook, stirring occasionally, until the rice is tender but still firm. (The ends of the grains may split; that's fine.) This can take from 30 to 50 minutes, depending on your wild rice. Drain the rice and set it aside in a bowl to cool.

3. Heat the butter in a small skillet over medium-low heat until the butter is foaming. Stir in the celery, ham, and scallions, reduce the heat to low and cover the pan. Cook, stirring occasionally, until the celery is tender, about 10 minutes.

4. Meanwhile, pour enough cranberry juice over the cherries in a small saucepan to cover them completely. Bring to a boil, let stand one minute, then drain.

5. Scrape the celery mixture into the wild rice. Add the drained cherries and walnuts and toss the stuffing ingredients together until well blended. Season the stuffing with salt and pepper to taste.

6. Spoon the stuffing into the quails, tamping it very lightly into the cavities. If your quail are semi-boneless, it is easier to stuff them if you lie them breast side up and lift the breast meat by pinching the skin over the breast and pulling up. Set each quail on the smoker rack as you go and plump it back into a neat shape—especially important if you are working with semi-boneless quail. Set up the smoker using the wood chips and smoke the quails according to the directions for Cornish game hens on page 99 until an instant-read thermometer inserted in the thickest part of the thigh near the bone registers 160°F. Serve hot.

seafood

Salmon Fillets and Steaks

The tremendous quantity of farm-raised salmon in the market has meant a steady supply and reasonable prices for what has become America's favorite fish. But I urge you to search out wild Alaskan salmon in warmer months. Their flavor, which varies from species to species, runs from the mild Coho to the richer and almost meaty King. Much of the Alaskan salmon you're likely to find in your market is frozen at sea—FAS in the trade. There is nothing wrong with this, providing the salmon was kept frozen through handling and defrosted slowly.

How Many? Up to four 10-ounce fillets or steaks will fit on the smoker rack at one time. Choose thick steaks or fillets, about 1¼ inches, when possible.

How Long? Until the thickest part is warm and slightly opaque (for a "medium" fillet); 14 to 18 minutes after closing the smoker lid for a 1¼-inch fillet; a few minutes longer for a fully cooked fillet/steak.

Which Wood? Milder woods like alder, cherry, and even maple work nicely with salmon. Start with 1½ to 2 tablespoons wood per batch.

Season the fillets or steaks with ½ to ¾ teaspoon kosher salt and ¼ teaspoon freshly ground black pepper each.

Check 1¼-inch fillets for doneness at 14 minutes, thinner ones sooner.

Serve smoked salmon with just about anything from tender green vegetables seasoned with butter and toasted almonds to a nice, crisp green salad. They are delicious topped with **Mango Salsa** (page 23), or served with just about any rice preparation you can think of. Or turn to these recipes for a little inspiration:

Smoked Salmon Gone to Heaven (page 144)

Fettuccine with Smoked Salmon, Peas, and Leeks (page 146)

NOTE: Run your hand lightly over the surface of the salmon fillets to feel for any bones. These bones can be removed with a sturdy pair of tweezers by grasping the tip of the bone that protrudes from the salmon and tugging firmly. They are also quite easy to pluck out after the salmon has been smoked.

Cod or Haddock Fillet

How Many? Up to six 8-ounce fillets will fit on the smoker rack at one time.

How Long? Until the flesh at the center of the fillet is barely opaque (for a "medium" fillet); about 14 minutes after closing the smoker lid. For a fillet that is evenly firm and opaque, smoke a minute or two longer.

Which Wood? 1 tablespoon of mild-flavored wood chips, like alder or apple.

Season the fillets with a generous amount of kosher salt and freshly ground black pepper, then rub them lightly with olive oil. Or, if you like, rub them with a seasoned lemon oil that will flavor and moisten them: For each fillet, stir 1 teaspoon olive oil, ½ teaspoon lemon juice, ½ teaspoon salt, and a large pinch of ground black pepper together in a small bowl. Rub gently into all sides.

Serve smoked cod or haddock with scalloped potatoes, macaroni and cheese, or couscous with a side of broccoli. Use leftover smoked cod or haddock fillets in **MV Fish Cakes** (page 159).

Unlike salmon or bluefish, which provide their own built-in supply of flavorful oils, cod and haddock fillets are quite lean. Rubbing them with a little oil helps keep the outside from drying out. A drizzle of olive oil or a pat of butter after they come out of the smoker wouldn't hurt either.

Bluefish or Mackerel Fillet

Members of these oil-rich families make excellent candidates for smoking. If you find very fresh Spanish mackerel (look for it in the late summer) or, better yet, know someone who catches them, they are absolutely delicious when smoked. Some people claim they don't like bluefish or mackerel, because they are too "fishy." Maybe those folks haven't had a really fresh specimen, or maybe they've never tried this simple trick: with a small paring knife, cut out the dark strip of flesh that runs down the center of the fillet. That darker flesh contains a lot of the fish's oil and, therefore, flavor.

How Many? Up to two 1¼ pound fillets will fit on the smoker rack at one time.

How Long? Until the thickest part of the fillet is opaque and firm at its center; 20 to 25 minutes after closing the smoker lid.

Which Wood? 1½ tablespoons oak or cherry wood chips or 1 tablespoon hickory wood chips.

Trim away the darker flesh (see left), if you like, as well as bones that run along the thinner (belly) part of the fillet.

Season simply with a generous sprinkling of kosher salt and freshly ground black pepper or stir 2 teaspoons light brown sugar, 1 teaspoon kosher salt, and ½ teaspoon freshly ground black pepper together in a bowl. (This is enough to season 2 pounds of fillets.) Rub the seasoning mix into the flesh side of the fillet. Let seasoned fillets sit in the refrigerator for 30 minutes or so to absorb the seasoning. Pat them dry before smoking, but don't wipe off the seasoning.

Start the fillets skin side down on the smoker rack.

Check the fillets for doneness after they have been smoking for 16 minutes.

Serve the fillets warm or at room temperature with buttered corn, a mixed green salad, and boiled potatoes.

Use flaked leftover fish in:

MV Fish Cakes (page 159)

Smoked Trout and Chive Cream Cheese Spread (in place of the trout) (page 32)

Swordfish or Tuna Steaks

How Many? Up to four 10-ounce tuna or swordfish steaks, each about 1 to 1¼ inches thick, will fit on the smoker rack at one time.

How Long? For a rare (pink, cool center) 1¼-inch tuna steak, about 18 minutes. For a fully cooked 1 to 1¼ inches tuna or swordfish steak, 22 to 25 minutes after closing the smoker lid.

Which Wood? Try 1 tablespoon alder or apple wood chips for a milder flavor; 1 tablespoon hickory or mesquite wood chips for a more pronounced flavor.

Season the steaks with 1 teaspoon kosher salt and ¼ teaspoon freshly ground black pepper each.

Check the steaks for doneness after they have been smoking for 16 minutes.

Serve smoked swordfish or tuna steaks with **Mango Salsa** (page 23) or **Fresh Tomato Salsa** (page 22). Stick with basics, like buttered corn on the cob and a fresh tomato salad in summer; buttered string beans and roasted new potatoes in winter.

If you like your tuna steaks rare—still cool and virtually uncooked in the center—you'll have to search out or cut steaks that are at least 1¼ inches thick. Steaks thinner than that will overcook by the time they absorb a lovely smoky flavor. I personally like swordfish steaks cooked though, but still perfectly moist, so thickness isn't as crucial there. Still, to keep the steaks from drying out, choose steaks no less than ¾ inch thick.

Whole Trout

How Many? Up to three 12-ounce whole trout will fit on the smoker rack at one time.

How Long? Until the meat along the backbone close to the head is opaque (insert the tip of a small knife to check); about 22 minutes after closing the smoker lid for an 11 to 12-ounce trout; about 25 minutes for a 13 to 14-ounce trout.

Which Wood? As with most seafood, alder and cherry wood chips are safe bets. Use 1½ to 2 tablespoons, depending on your preference for smokiness.

Trim the very ends of the tail if the trout are too long for the smoker. Otherwise, leave them as is. Some retailers will sell a whole, boneless trout, which makes serving easier, but skinning a smoked trout and separating the fillets from the bones is a very simple affair (see below).

Season the inside and outside of the trout generously with salt and pepper. If you like, lay a slice or two of lemon and a few branches of fresh thyme inside the body cavity.

Check the fish for doneness as described above after 20 minutes. If the underside is considerably darker than the top after about 12 minutes of smoking, flip the fish and continue cooking.

Serve the trout right out of the smoker with simple accompaniments like rice pilaf and buttered string beans tossed with almonds. Or, cool them completely to room temperature and remove the fillets. To fillet smoked trout, run a small sharp knife along the backbone to cut through the skin. Lift off the skin from the top fillet or leave it on if you like. With the help of the knife, gently lift the top fillet free of the bones. Turn the fish over and repeat. Use smoked trout in:

Smoked Trout and Chive Cream Cheese Spread (page 32)

Smoked Trout Fillets with Baby Greens and Horse-radish Whipped Cream (page 33)

NOTE: To smoke trout fillets, set them skin side down on the smoker rack and smoke just until cooked through and they begin to flake, 12 to 15 minutes, depending on thickness.

Shrimp

Shopping for shrimp can be an enlightening experience. One store's colossal is another store's large. The solution: look for the count—in other words, how many shrimp per pound—as the only accurate indicator of the size of shrimp you are buying. This is usually expressed as a range, like "16-20," which means there are between sixteen and twenty shrimp per pound. Naturally, the fewer shrimp per pound, the larger (and more expensive) the shrimp. If this information isn't displayed along with the price—as it usually is in a supermarket—ask the person behind the counter. They will always be able to supply the answer. I don't recommend smoking anything smaller than 21-25s; smaller shrimp will overcook before they pick up a smoky kick.

How Many? About 1½ pounds of shrimp will fit on the smoker rack at one time.

How Long? Until uniformly opaque at the center; depending on size (see left); about 12 minutes after closing the smoker lid for 21-25s, 14 minutes for 16-20s or 18 minutes for U-15s (under 15 per pound).

Which Wood? 1½ to 2 tablespoons of alder, hickory, or cherry wood chips.

Peel the shells from the shrimp, removing the tails if you plan to use the shrimp in another dish, like a seafood salad or pasta. Leave the tails on if you plan to serve the shrimp with a dip. **Cut** along the length of the curved back of each shrimp with a paring knife just deep enough to reveal the sand vein, if there is one (not all shrimp have them). Pull out and discard the sand vein, then rinse the shrimp briefly under cold water and pat them dry with paper towels.

Season one pound of shelled shrimp with 1¼ teaspoons kosher salt and ¼ teaspoon freshly ground black pepper. Add other seasonings, like grated lemon zest, dried tarragon, or a sprinkling of paprika as you see fit.

Check the shrimp for doneness after about 10 minutes. If those closer to the edges of the rack are cooking more slowly than those in the center, change the positions so the shrimp cook evenly.

Serve smoked shrimp on their own or with your favorite cocktail sauce, adding a little squeeze of fresh lemon or lime juice. Or pile them on a platter with a small bowl of **Green Goddess Sauce** (page 17) in the center. Toss smoked shrimp into a Caesar salad or green salad, or use them in **Bow Tie Pasta Salad with Smoked Shrimp and Cherry Tomatoes** (page 85).

Mussels

How Many? Up to one pound of mussels will fit on the smoker rack at one time.

How Long? Until the shells are opened and the meat is opaque but not tough, about 12 minutes after closing the smoker lid.

Which Wood? 1 to 1½ tablespoons of alder, cherry, or hickory wood chips.

Swish the mussels vigorously in a large bowl or sinkful of cold water. Drain them thoroughly. **Trim** the beards, if any, which stick out of the flat side of the shell by holding the mussel firmly in one hand and tugging on the beard with the other. Clean and beard the mussels just before smoking them.

Start the mussels with the hinged edge—rounded, not straight—of the shell set between the rungs of the smoker rack. This keeps the mussels stable as they smoke and keeps more of the juices inside the shell as the mussels open.

Check the mussels for doneness after 10 minutes.

Serve the mussels warm from the smoker with melted butter and thin lemon wedges. Lift them gently to keep as much of the juice in the shell as possible. Or pluck them from the shell and use them in seafood salads, as part of a chilled seafood appetizer platter, or in:

Smoky Mussel Chowder (page 72)

NOTE: 1 pound of mussels in the shell yields about ⅔ cup smoked mussel meat.

Cultivated mussels aren't mussels with an appreciation of the fine arts, but mussels that are farmed for the table. They are grown in a controlled environment and are, usually, cleaner and plumper than wild mussels. Look for cultivated mussels in two-pound bags in many fish shops and supermarkets. Cultivated mussels also lack the wiry beards that anchor wild mussels to underwater rocks. A good thing, since the beards can be a pain to remove.

Oysters on the Half Shell

Some folks won't touch a raw oyster with a ten-foot pole; others won't eat them any other way. I propose a third approach: smoke them lightly to keep their briny goodness and plump texture intact. I choose Atlantic oysters—those with fairly sturdy elongated or oval shells—and avoid small or thin-shelled oysters like Pacific oysters and Belons, respectively. See the upcoming box for a crash course in shucking oysters.

How Many? Up to 12 oysters on the half shell will fit on the smoker rack at one time.

How Long? Until the oysters are very lightly colored and firm, but still plump and moist, 9 minutes over the heat after closing the smoker lid and about 6 minutes off the heat with the smoker lid closed.

Which Wood? 1 tablespoon of alder, corncob, or cherry wood chips. Any more than that won't have a chance to burn in the limited time the oysters smoke.

Start the oysters over medium heat and lower the heat slightly once the smoker lid is closed.

Check the oysters for doneness after they have been off the heat 5 minutes.

Serve the oysters in all their nakedness right out of the smoker, or drizzle them with melted butter and pass lemon wedges, a pepper mill, and a bottle of hot red pepper sauce separately. Prepare your favorite stuffed oyster recipe with smoked oysters instead, or fold a few into a spinach omelet. Or try them in **Oysters Vanderbilt** (page 36).

NOTE: I love the mild flavor of home-smoked oysters. If you like the heavy-smoked flavor and drier texture of canned smoked oysters, increase the wood to 2½ tablespoons and the smoking time to 25 minutes.

TO SHUCK OYSTERS

Shucking oysters isn't the easiest task in the kitchen, but it most certainly is one where practice makes perfect. Start by scrubbing the oyster shells thoroughly with a stiff brush under cold running water. While they are draining in a colander, set up the smoker and insert the rack.

Take a look at an oyster: there is one cupped shell and one more or less flat shell. Always shuck oysters with the flat side up, so you discard the flat shell and leave the cupped shell to hold the oyster and its juices. If you are right-handed, pad your left palm with several layers of kitchen towel and use it to hold the oyster firmly in place on the work surface. Look at the hinged (i.e., narrower) end of the oyster. You can usually spot an opening that will serve as your point of entry. Wiggle the tip of an oyster knife, church-key style bottle opener, or a small screwdriver into this opening and twist it, separating the top and bottom shells. You'll know when this happens: you will feel the tight bond between shells loosen dramatically. If you are straining too hard to pry the shells apart, take a better look for the opening or set that oyster aside and try another. With a few shucked oysters under your belt you'll tackle this problem a little more confidently.

Once you've separated the shells, run a thin-bladed, not-too-sharp knife all along the top shell, pressing the knife blade as close as possible to the shell to avoid cutting into the oyster. Discard the top shell. Run the knife blade underneath the bottom shell, again pressing it tightly to the shell to keep the oyster whole. Set the oyster shell, with as much of the juice as possible, on the smoker rack.

If you don't want to shuck oysters and your fish seller won't shuck them and save you the shells, consider this option: Buy shucked oysters and smoke them, three to a dish, in small (about 3-inch) heatproof baking dishes. Increase the smoking time for oysters smoked in this way by a few minutes.

Smoked Salmon Gone to Heaven

In this simple recipe, a plump, juicy salmon steak sits on top of tender white beans and sweet leeks. The beans and leeks are given a last minute zing with golden-brown garlic and fresh parsley. This is perfect winter food—warm and cozy, not too filling, and incredibly easy. The beans are also excellent served with sea scallops or jumbo shrimp. Or next to grilled pork chops, under lamb kabobs, alongside a nice roast chicken, spooned over thick slices of grilled whole wheat country bread . . . You get the idea.

MAKES 2 SERVINGS

Two 1¼-inch-thick smoked salmon fillets or steaks

3 tablespoons extra virgin olive oil

1 tablespoon unsalted butter

2 medium leeks, cleaned (see page 61) and sliced ½ inch thick (about 2 cups)

Kosher salt

One 19-ounce can cannellini beans or white beans, drained and rinsed

1 cup homemade or canned reduced-sodium chicken broth

3 or 4 garlic cloves, peeled and thinly sliced

3 to 4 tablespoons chopped fresh flat-leaf parsley or thinly sliced scallion

Freshly ground black pepper

1. Smoke the salmon according to the directions on page 134.

2. While the salmon is smoking, heat 1 tablespoon of the olive oil and the butter in a large skillet until the butter is foaming. Stir in the leeks, season them lightly with salt and cook, stirring, until they are wilted, about 4 minutes. Gently stir in the beans, toss a few times, and pour in the chicken broth. Bring to a boil, adjust the heat to simmering and simmer, uncovered, until there is enough syrupy liquid left to generously coat the beans, about 8 minutes. If the salmon is done to your likeness before the beans are ready, remove the smoker from the heat and open the top an inch or so.

3. Heat the remaining 2 tablespoons oil in a very small skillet over medium-low heat. Scatter the garlic over the oil and cook, shaking the pan, until it is a very pale golden brown, about 2 minutes. Remove immediately from the heat and stir in the parsley, then stir the whole thing into the beans. Taste

the beans and add salt and pepper as you like. Divide the beans between two warm shallow bowls. Top each with a piece of salmon and serve at once.

NOTE: The beans—without the finishing touch of garlic and parsley—can be prepared up to an hour in advance. Rewarm them over low heat just before serving and add additional chicken broth or water to return them to their original juiciness.

Fettuccine with Smoked Salmon, Peas, and Leeks

There is just enough rosy-pink sauce to coat the strands of pasta. If you find the pasta a little dry, spoon in hot water or, better yet, some of the pasta cooking water until the pasta is coated lightly with sauce.

MAKES 4 MAIN COURSE SERVINGS

Two 8-ounce smoked salmon fillets or steaks

Kosher salt

3 tablespoons olive oil or unsalted butter

2 medium leeks, white and light green parts only, cleaned (see page 61) and sliced ½ inch thick

1 cup frozen baby peas, defrosted and drained

1 tablespoon tomato paste

½ cup homemade or canned reduced-sodium chicken broth

½ cup heavy cream

2 teaspoons chopped fresh tarragon or ¾ teaspoon dried tarragon

12 ounces fettuccine (three-quarters of a 1-pound package)

3 tablespoons chopped flat-leaf parsley or chives

Freshly ground black pepper

1. Smoke the salmon according to the directions on page 134 and cool it to room temperature. (This can be done up to two days in advance.) Remove any skin and shred the salmon coarsely, keeping an eye out for bones as you go. Set aside.

2. Bring a large pot of salted water to a boil over high heat.

3. Meanwhile, heat the olive oil in a medium skillet over medium heat. Stir in the leeks and peas, cover the skillet and cook, stirring often, until the leeks are tender, about 8 minutes. Stir in the tomato paste and cook, stirring, until you can smell it. Pour in the broth and cream, raise the heat to high and bring to a boil. Stir in the tarragon and adjust the heat so the sauce is at a gentle boil and cook until reduced by about half.

4. While the sauce is cooking, stir the fettuccine into the boiling water. Cook, stirring occasionally, until the fettuccine

is al dente, about 9 minutes. If the sauce is finished before the pasta is cooked, turn off the heat under the sauce and let it stand.

5. Ladle off and reserve about ½ cup of the pasta cooking water, then drain the pasta in a colander. Slide the fettuccine back into the pot and place the pot over medium-low heat. Scrape in the sauce with a rubber spatula and add the parsley and salmon. Bring to a gentle boil, season with pepper and, if necessary, salt. Cook until the salmon is heated through and there is just enough lightly thickened sauce to generously coat the pasta. If the pasta looks too dry, stir in some of the reserved pasta cooking water about 1 tablespoon at a time. Serve in warm bowls or on a warm platter.

Bronzed Sea Scallops with Chunky Tomato Vinaigrette

This is a summer dish for when seafood is king and tomatoes are at their best. You'll need nothing besides some buttered string beans or peas to round out this dish, but some saffron rice would be nice, too.

MAKES 4 SERVINGS

I large, juicy, ripe tomato

Kosher salt

Freshly ground black pepper

⅓ cup extra virgin olive oil

I tablespoon chopped fresh thyme leaves, or 3 tablespoons shredded fresh basil, or both

I½ pounds large smoked sea scallops (about 16), preferably dry (see Note)

I½ tablespoons alder, cherry, or corn cob wood chips

2 tablespoons red wine vinegar

1. Bring a large saucepan of water to a boil. Cut the core from the tomato and cut a small X in the bottom with a paring knife. Slip the tomato into the water and cook just until the skin begins to peel away from the X. This will take from 15 to 25 seconds, depending on the tomato. Scoop the tomato out of the water with a slotted spoon and hold it under cold running water for a few seconds. Drain the tomato thoroughly and peel it. Cut the tomato in half along its equator and squeeze the seeds out of each half. Cut the tomato into ½-inch pieces and place them in a small bowl. Season lightly with salt and pepper and toss gently with the olive oil and herbs. The tomatoes can be prepared up to an hour or so in advance. Keep them at room temperature.

2. Pat the scallops dry with paper towels. Season generously with salt and pepper. Set up the smoker with the wood chips of your choice and smoke the scallops according to the directions on page 4 until they are barely opaque at the center and spring back gently when poked with your finger, about 15 minutes after closing the lid.

3. While the scallops are smoking, finish the vinaigrette: Pour the vinegar into the bowl with the tomato, give every-

thing a gentle toss and taste, adding salt and pepper if necessary. The tomatoes will have given off some of their juices, which will add to the flavor of the dressing.

4. Spoon the vinaigrette onto serving plates and top the vinaigrette with the scallops. Serve immediately.

NOTE: Most scallops, after they are harvested and shucked at sea, are immersed in a preservative solution which, unfortunately, they absorb. These "wet" scallops develop a soft texture and, because of the excess water, are very difficult to brown when cooking. "Dry" scallops are shucked and shipped without any such solution; they will taste sweeter, have a firmer texture, and brown beautifully. It is fairly easy to tell the two apart: wet scallops will be uniformly white; dry scallops will range in color from very pale pink to ivory to white and shades in between. Dry scallops will also hold their individual shape better when raw than wet scallops. Choose dry scallops whenever possible.

Tea-Smoked Shrimp and Asparagus Stir-Fry

MAKES 4 SERVINGS

1 pound medium (about 25 to the pound) smoked shrimp

3 tablespoons loose green tea

1 pound asparagus with stalks slightly thicker than a pencil (about 20 stalks)

One 8-ounce stalk broccoli

¼ cup homemade or canned reduced-sodium chicken broth, or water

2 tablespoons soy sauce

2 tablespoons oyster sauce

2 tablespoons peanut or vegetable oil

2 scallions, trimmed and minced

3 quarter size slices peeled fresh ginger, minced

3 garlic cloves, minced

8 medium (about 3-inch) shiitake mushroom caps, sliced ¼ inch

1. Smoke the shrimp according to the directions on page 140, using the green tea in place of the wood chips. Cool them to room temperature. This may be done up to 1 hour in advance.

2. Prepare the remaining stir-fry ingredients: hold each stalk of asparagus with one hand about halfway down the stalk from the tip and the other by the stalk end. Bend the stalk away from you till it snaps. This is the easiest way to remove the tougher part of the stalk. Discard the tough ends and peel the stalks with a vegetable peeler up to about an inch below the tip. Cut off the tips then cut the stalks into 1-inch lengths on the diagonal. Cut the florets from the broccoli and chop them coarsely. Peel the stems and cut into ¼-inch dice. Stir the broth, soy sauce, and oyster sauce together in a small bowl.

3. Heat the oil in a seasoned wok or large, heavy nonstick skillet over medium-high heat until the oil is shimmering. Add the scallions, ginger, and garlic and stir until you can

smell the garlic, about 30 seconds. Scatter the asparagus and broccoli into the wok and immediately start tossing to distribute the seasonings and cook the asparagus evenly. Cook until the vegetables turn bright green, about 1 minute. Add the shiitakes and cook, stirring constantly, until the mushrooms are wilted and the vegetables are crisp-tender, about 4 minutes.

4. When the vegetables are crisp-tender, add the shrimp and pour in the broth mixture. Continue stirring until the sauce is thickened enough to lightly coat the vegetables and the shrimp are heated through. Scoop the contents of the wok onto a platter and serve immediately.

Smoked Cod with Bacon and Cabbage

There is a little rhyme that I've heard in all kinds of kitchens and from all kinds of cooks: "Salt and fat. That's where it's at." While your doctor may not agree with this sentiment, no one can argue with the fact that we love these things. The small amount of butter swirled into this dish in the last minute adds richness, and the sweet-smokiness of the bacon nicely complements the lightly smoked cod. You can, however, make a lighter and delicious version of this dish by eliminating one or both of these ingredients. As always, I make suggestions for the level of smokiness here, but let your own taste be your guide.

MAKES 2 SERVINGS

2 tablespoons olive oil

1 ounce slab bacon, cut into 1 × ¼ × ¼-inch strips (about 3 tablespoons) or 2 slices thick-sliced bacon, cut crosswise into ½-inch strips, optional

2 medium leeks, white and light green parts only, cleaned (see page 61) and cut into ½-inch strips (about 2 cups)

Half a small head savoy cabbage (about 2 pounds), outer leaves and core removed, leaves cut into 1-inch strips, or 8 cups cleaned Swiss chard (see Note)

One 14-ounce can reduced-sodium chicken broth

Kosher salt

Freshly ground black pepper

1½ tablespoons alder or cherry wood chips

Two 8-ounce smoked cod or haddock fillets, each about 1 inch thick

2 tablespoons unsalted butter, optional

1. Heat the oil in a heavy, large skillet over medium-low heat. Add the bacon, if using. Cook, turning often, until lightly browned but still quite soft, about 5 minutes (a little less if you're using bacon strips). Scoop out the bacon pieces with a slotted spoon and set them aside. Increase the heat to medium; stir in the leeks and cook, stirring often, until the leeks are lightly browned, about 5 minutes. Stir in a large handful of cabbage and cook until it has wilted enough to add another. Continue until all the cabbage is added, then pour in the chicken broth. Increase the heat to high and bring the broth to a boil. Cook until the cabbage is tender and the broth is almost completely evaporated, about 12 minutes. Season with salt and pepper. The dish can be prepared to this point

up to an hour in advance. Remove the skillet from the heat and keep it covered until needed.

2. Set up the smoker using the wood chips and smoke the cod fillets according to directions on page 135.

3. About 5 minutes before the fillets are done smoking, reheat the cabbage. Remove the pan from the heat and stir in the butter, if using. Divide the cabbage between two plates and center a fillet over each.

NOTE: If you opt for the chard instead of the cabbage, prepare it as follows: Trim off any wilted or yellow parts of the leaves. Cut away the stems. You can slice the stems thinly and cook them a minute or two before adding the leaves but, frankly, I am not that fond of them. Stack several of the leaves on a cutting board and cut them into rough 2-inch pieces. Wash them in plenty of cool water and drain thoroughly.

Preserved Tuna, Sicilian Style

Many Sicilians still prepare this delicacy in quantity. They preserve it by boiling the jars of tuna as you would fruit preserves. Here, I offer a simpler version that, because the tuna is completely submerged in oil, will last in the refrigerator up to 10 days. The tuna is delicious plucked right from the oil with just a sprinkling of coarse sea salt, either on its own or as part of an antipasto platter. Or use it in the Tuna and White Bean Salad on page 82. If you can find fatty tuna, known as *toro* to Japanese sushi chefs, use it here. Its richer meat will yield a silky, tender texture.

MAKES ABOUT 2 CUPS

(can be easily doubled)

One 10-ounce smoked tuna steak

2 sprigs fresh rosemary

2 bay leaves

2 cups extra virgin olive oil, or as needed

1. Smoke the tuna according to the directions on page 137 until well-done (no trace of pink remains in the center), about 25 minutes. Remove from the smoker and cool to room temperature.

2. Drop the rosemary sprigs into a small saucepan of boiling water. Cook until they turn bright green, about 20 seconds. Drain them immediately, then pat them dry with paper towels.

3. Flake the tuna with your fingers into pieces roughly 1½ inches long. Spread them out on paper towels to dry completely, picking off any dark pieces, if there are any, as you go.

4. Transfer the tuna pieces to a 1-quart glass jar with a tight-fitting lid. Drop in the bay leaves and rosemary. Pour in enough olive oil to completely cover the fish and herbs. Refrigerate at least three days before using. Let the tuna and oil come to room temperature before serving. The tuna will keep refrigerated up to ten days.

NOTE: Whenever you use fresh herbs to season oil they must be cooked briefly to eliminate the possibility of botulism.

Chef Walsh's Swordfish with Radicchio and Papaya Salad

1 small head (about 4 ounces) radicchio

2 heads Belgian endive

1 Fuji or Granny Smith apple

2 tablespoons fresh lime juice, plus a little more for the apples

1 ripe but semi-firm papaya

4 smoked swordfish steaks

3 tablespoons chopped fresh cilantro

2 tablespoons orange juice

1 teaspoon kosher salt, or to taste

¼ teaspoon freshly ground black pepper

⅓ cup extra virgin olive oil

1. Cut the head of radicchio in half through the core. Peel off any wilted or discolored outer leaves, then pull off individual leaves from the head. Tear the leaves into pieces that are more or less 2 inches wide. Cut the endive lengthwise into quarters, cut out the core pieces, and separate the leaves. Wash the radicchio and endive and dry them well, preferably in a salad spinner. Transfer the greens to a large bowl.

2. Wash the apple and cut it into quarters. Cut out the core from each section, then cut the apple into strips about ¼ × ¼ inch. Toss the apples with just enough lime juice to coat them to prevent them from darkening. Cut the papaya in half, and scoop out and discard the seeds. Peel the halves, cut them in half crosswise, then cut them into ½ × ½-inch strips. Scatter the fruits over the greens. The salad may be prepared up to a few hours in advance. Refrigerate it, covered with a damp paper towel, and bring the salad to room temperature before smoking the swordfish.

3. Smoke the swordfish according to the directions on page 137.

A decade and a half ago, I had one of the best experiences of my professional chef career. I worked with Brendan Walsh during the opening of Arizona 206, the Manhattan restaurant that redefined the cuisine of the American Southwest. Chef Walsh devised a grilled salmon dish that was served over a salad of radicchio, papaya, and jicama—a crunchy root vegetable with an appley flavor. This is my take on that dish—citrusy cilantro vinaigrette and all. I love this blend of bitter (radicchio and endive) and sweet (papaya and apple), with tart (lime and orange juice). If you are not a radicchio fan, substitute a milder green, like Boston lettuce.

MAKES 4 SERVINGS

4. While the fish is smoking, whisk the cilantro, 2 tablespoons lime juice, orange juice, salt, and pepper together in a mixing bowl until the salt is dissolved. Continue whisking while pouring in the olive oil. Taste the dressing and add salt if necessary.

5. A few minutes before the swordfish is done smoking, toss the salad with the dressing. Divide the salad among 4 dinner plates, mounding it slightly. Top the salad with swordfish hot from the smoker and serve immediately.

Shrimp and Sausage Jambalaya

¼ cup vegetable oil

3 links (about 10 ounces) smoked hot Italian sausages (page 169) or store-bought andouille or spicy garlic sausages, cut into 2-inch lengths

8 ounces diced (½-inch) smoked pork tenderloin (page 163) or store-bought smoked pork butt (about 1½ cups)

2 medium yellow onions, diced (about 3 cups)

2 celery stalks, trimmed and diced (about 1 cup)

1 large red pepper, cored, seeded, and diced (about 1 cup)

1 teaspoon kosher salt, plus more for seasoning the vegetables

1 teaspoon dried thyme

¼ teaspoon cayenne pepper

¼ teaspoon allspice

1 cup canned diced Italian tomatoes with their liquid

2 bay leaves

2 cups long-grain rice

¾ pound large (about 25 per pound) shrimp, peeled and deveined (see Note)

¼ cup chopped fresh flat-leaf parsley

3 scallions, trimmed and sliced

Jambalaya, like the Pulled Pork on page 170, is one of those regional American dishes that can spark a passionate argument or poetic description every time it is mentioned. Like the Pulled Pork, this recipe is my own interpretation of a classic—one that is suited to your home smoker. This recipe is perfect for using a small piece of leftover smoked pork tenderloin (page 163) or a few extra links of smoked spicy sausages. If neither are on hand and you don't want to make them, alternates are offered here. Don't look for fluffy, individual grains of rice in a jambalaya; the texture is as dense as the flavor is rich.

1. Heat half the oil in an 8-quart Dutch oven or heavy pot over medium heat. Add the sausages and pork and cook, stirring often, until they are well browned on all sides, about 8 minutes. Scoop them out with a slotted spoon and drain them on a paper towel-lined plate.

2. Add the remaining oil to the pot. Add the onions, celery, and red pepper, season them lightly with salt and cook, stirring, until wilted and lightly browned, about 12 minutes. Add the thyme, cayenne, and allspice.

MAKES 6 GENEROUS SERVINGS

3. Pour in 4 cups water and the tomatoes with their liquid. Bring to a boil. Drop in the bay leaves and season the liquid with 1 teaspoon salt. Stir in the rice, bring the liquid back to a boil, then adjust the heat so the liquid is at a gentle simmer. Cover the pot and cook 15 minutes.

4. Stir in the shrimp, parsley, and scallions. Taste a little of the mixture and add salt if necessary. Re-cover the pot and cook until the shrimp are cooked through and the rice is tender, but still firm, about 10 minutes. Remove the pot from the heat and let stand 5 minutes before serving.

NOTE: If you would like to up the smokiness of the jambalaya, smoke the shrimp lightly before adding them: Set up the smoker using 1 tablespoon alder or cherry wood chips. Smoke the peeled shrimp 8 minutes, remove them from the smoker and cool them to room temperature. The shrimp will be quite undercooked. They will finish cooking in the jambalaya.

MV Fish Cakes

1 small (8-ounce) russet
  potato

2 tablespoons vegetable oil

2 tablespoons unsalted butter

1 small yellow onion, finely
  diced (about ⅔ cup)

1 small celery stalk, trimmed
  and finely diced (about ⅓
  cup)

Kosher salt

Freshly ground black pepper

½ teaspoon dried thyme

8 ounces smoked fish
  (salmon, cod, bluefish,
  or mackerel, or any
  combination), flaked
  (about 1½ cups)

2 tablespoons breadcrumbs

1 egg, well beaten

1. Pour enough water over the potato in a medium saucepan to cover it by 3 inches or so. Bring to a boil and cook until the potato is barely tender when you poke it with a knife, about 25 minutes. Drain and let stand until cool enough to handle.

2. While the potato is cooking, heat 1 tablespoon of the oil and 1 tablespoon of the butter in a small skillet over medium-low heat until the butter is foaming. Stir in the onion and celery and cook until tender and lightly browned, about 10 minutes. Season with salt and pepper, stir in the thyme and remove from the heat.

3. Scrape off the potato peel and cut the potato into large dice. Toss the potato, cooked vegetables, fish, and bread-crumbs together in a medium bowl, breaking up the potatoes and fish slightly as you do. Season the mixture with salt and pepper, then stir in the beaten egg. Form the mixture into 4-inch cakes. The cakes can be prepared up to a day in advance and stored, uncooked, in the refrigerator.

My first job out of culinary school was in the kitchen of the Black Dog Tavern on Martha's Vineyard, where I cooked simple, fresh food for locals and tourists. The Black Dog's fish cakes, adapted here to use smoked fish instead of steamed, were a hit at breakfast served with eggs any style. We always sold out of fish cakes, no matter how many we made. You can use whatever type of fish you like. My favorite is bluefish.

MAKES 6 CAKES

4. Heat the remaining tablespoon each of butter and oil in a large skillet or on a griddle over medium-low heat. Cook the cakes, turning once, until heated through and the outsides are crispy brown, about 12 minutes. Serve hot.

NOTE: Whenever you cook foods that contain raw eggs, like these fish cakes, it is important to cook them thoroughly. That is why I call for relatively low heat and a longer cooking time. A fringe benefit of cooking the cakes slowly is an even, crispy, deep golden brown crust.

pork

Pork Chops

Choose thick—about $1\frac{1}{2}$ inches—chops for smoking. My personal favorites are from the front, or rib, half of the loin and resemble little T-bone steaks. You may brine the chops (see page II) if you like, but it isn't necessary.

How Many? Up to four $1\frac{1}{2}$-inch (12-ounce) pork chops will fit on the smoker rack at one time.

How Long? Until an instant-read thermometer inserted into the thickest part of the chop near the bone registers 145°F; 25 to 30 minutes after closing the smoker lid for a $1\frac{1}{2}$-inch-thick chop.

Which Wood? Try 2 to $2\frac{1}{2}$ tablespoons of hickory or oak wood chips or $1\frac{1}{2}$ to 2 tablespoons of corncob or apple wood chips.

Statistically, pork is safe to eat once it reaches an internal temperature of 137°F. I like to give a little leeway and suggest removing pork from the smoker when it reaches 145°F. The temperature will climb a degree or two after you take it out of the smoker. Pork cooked to that temperature retains a slight pink tint nearest the bone. If that makes you nervous—and it shouldn't—cook the pork to an internal temperature of 155°F.

Trim any excess fat from the edges of the chops before seasoning.

Season each 12-ounce chop with ¾ teaspoon kosher salt and a scant ½ teaspoon freshly ground black pepper. If possible, rub the chops with the seasoning several hours in advance and refrigerate them.

Check the chops for doneness after about 20 minutes; less time for thinner chops.

Serve smoked pork chops with sweet and sour red cabbage (the version on page 176 works beautifully) or applesauce. If you make homemade applesauce, prepare a batch substituting pear for some of the apples. I also like smoked pork chops with broccoli rabe or other bitter greens like chard or kale, cooked until tender with olive oil and garlic.

Pork Tenderloin

How Many? One or two 1¼-pound pork tenderloins will fit on the smoker rack at one time.

How Long? Until an instant-read thermometer inserted into the thickest part of the tenderloin registers 145°F; about 25 minutes from the time the smoker lid is closed.

Which Wood? 2 tablespoons alder or cherry wood chips or 4 to 5 teaspoons of hickory wood chips.

Trim any excess fat from the tenderloin(s), if you like. I leave it on; there is never all that much.

Season the pork with a generous rubbing of coarse salt and freshly ground black pepper or 4 teaspoons of the **Mushroom-Herb Rub** (page 27) or **Southwestern Rub** (page 28).

Check the tenderloin(s) for doneness with an instant-read thermometer after 20 minutes of cooking; the remaining cooking time will vary with the thickness and shape of the tenderloin.

Serve the pork tenderloins thinly sliced with **Mango Salsa** (page 23) or **Asian Slaw** (page 128) or use them in **Monster Minestrone** (page 60).

NOTE: If you'd like to make carving—and chewing—easier whenever you prepare pork tenderloins, cut away any silver skin, the grayish white membrane that covers a portion of the thicker end of the tenderloin: slip a small sharp knife underneath one end of the silver skin and, with a gentle sawing motion, remove it from the pork, cutting off as little meat as possible.

It is becoming harder to find pork tenderloins that are not packed in plastic, floating around in some kind of seasoned brine. I have nothing against brine (see page 11), but those pre-seasoned tenderloins have an odd, artificial taste that becomes odder when they're smoked. Look for pork tenderloins in their natural state.

Spareribs

Spareribs are one of the foods, like meat loaf, that spark a lively debate anytime it's brought up. I will not wade that deeply into the sparerib battle, but will offer what I think is definitively the best way to prepare spareribs in a stovetop smoker. Spareribs should be cooked before they are smoked (or grilled, for that matter). But simmering them, as is often recommended, leaches out flavor from the ribs and makes them waterlogged. Baking the ribs first in a thin barbecue sauce—the one on page 18 is ideal—tenderizes them and adds flavor instead of drawing it out. The baking takes about an hour and a half, but can be done up to two days in advance.

How Many? One 2½ to 3-pound rack of spareribs, cut in half crosswise, will fit on the smoker rack at one time.

Trim any excess layer of fat from the meaty side of the rack.

Season a 2½-pound rack of ribs with 1½ teaspoons kosher salt and ½ teaspoon freshly ground black pepper. If possible, rub the seasoning into the ribs and refrigerate them for up to a day before cooking.

Combo-Cooking: Before smoking the ribs as described below, tenderize them with a stint in the oven. Preheat the oven to 300°F. Spoon half a recipe of **Barbecue Sauce** (page 18) or 1 cup store-bought barbecue sauce over the bottom of a baking dish large enough to hold the two halves of the rack of ribs comfortably. If you are using a bottled barbecue sauce, thin it with water to the consistency of tomato juice. Set the rib pieces side by side over the sauce and spoon the remaining Barbecue Sauce or 1 more cup bottled sauce over them. Seal the dish tightly with aluminum foil and bake until the ribs are very tender, about 1½ hours. Cool completely before smoking. The ribs may be baked up to three days before smoking. Refrigerate them until needed and remove any solidified fat from the surface of the sauce.

Scrape excess sauce from the ribs into a small saucepan before smoking the ribs. Set the sauce aside. Just before the ribs are done smoking, rewarm the sauce over low heat. Brush the sauce over the smoked ribs or pass it separately at the table.

Which Wood? 2 tablespoons of either hickory or mesquite wood chips are ideal for pork ribs. If you like the twang of corncob chips, use an equal amount of those.

Start the ribs meaty side up on the rack.

How Long? Until the meat pulls easily from the bone, 30 to 40 minutes after closing the smoker lid. **Serve** the ribs with any of the coleslaw variations on page 90 and/or your favorite potato salad.

Baby Back Ribs

How Many? One larger rack of baby backs (around 1¾ pounds) or two smaller (about 1 pound) racks will fit on the smoker rack at one time.

How Long? Until an instant-read thermometer inserted into the thickest part of the meat away from the bone registers 160°F, about 40 minutes from the time you close the smoker lid. Finishing the ribs off as described below will add another 5 to 15 minutes to the cooking time.

Which Wood? Go for the gusto with 2 to 3 tablespoons of mesquite or hickory. Baby back ribs require very little preparation, but if you like, **trim** any surface fat from the ribs before rubbing them with seasoning.

Season each rack by rubbing 1 teaspoon kosher salt and, if you like, ¼ to ½ teaspoon chili powder into the meatier side, or use the **Southwestern Rub** on page 28.

Check the ribs for doneness with an instant-read thermometer after 30 minutes.

Serve smoked baby backs right out of the smoker with your favorite homemade or store-bought barbecue sauce.

Combo-Cooking: For a dynamite flavor and crackling texture, roast or grill baby back ribs briefly after they emerge from the smoker. In either case, pick one of the glazes or sauces that follow and brush it over the meaty side of the ribs two or three times while they're in the oven or on the grill.

To roast baby back ribs, brush them with the glaze of your choice. Lay them meaty side up on a foil-lined baking sheet and bake them in a preheated 450°F oven until sizzling and well-browned, about 15 minutes. Brush them with more glaze once or twice as they roast.

Unlike whole racks of spareribs, baby back ribs can be smoked from their raw state. They will be pleasantly chewy, not fall-off-the-bone-tender like the preceding spareribs. To make life easier, the ribs can be smoked up to three days before you roast or grill them. Keep refrigerated until needed. Allow a few minutes extra finishing time for refrigerated ribs.

To grill baby backs, brush them with the glaze of your choice and sear them over a hot gas or charcoal grill until well-browned and crisp, about 5 minutes. Brush them occasionally with glaze as they grill, but take care to turn them often to prevent the glaze from burning.

NOTE: Chili powder means different things to different people. In its purest sense, it is one kind of dried chile pepper ground to a powder. These chile powders are easy to spot because the labels will refer to them as ancho chili powder, pequin chili powder, and so on, according to the type of chile used. Most people relate to chili powder as a blend of ground chiles, salt, and other spices used to season chili. I suggest you start with a single-chile powder and season the dish to taste with whatever else you like. But if you have a chili powder seasoning blend you like, stick with it.

Baby Back Ribs with . . .

. . . Carolina-Style "Mop" Sauce

So-called because the meat is mopped with the sauce during the final stages of a long, slow cooking process, mop sauce is a staple of Carolina-style barbecue.

⅓ cup white vinegar

1½ teaspoons kosher salt

2 to 3 teaspoons crushed red pepper flakes

2 teaspoons sugar, optional

1. Stir all the ingredients and ¼ cup water together in a small skillet or saucepan over low heat just until the salt is dissolved. Cool to room temperature.

2. Baste the ribs several times as they roast or grill using about half the sauce. Pass the remaining sauce separately.

Each of the sauces makes about twice the amount you'll need for basting. Pass the remaining sauce at the table for dunking.

MAKES ABOUT I CUP

. . . Quickie Teriyaki Glaze

Because of the sugar, this teriyaki glaze will brown quickly. Keep an eye on the ribs as they grill or roast to prevent them from burning.

⅔ cup soy sauce

2 tablespoons light or dark brown sugar

2 tablespoons sake or dry white wine

2 tablespoons white wine or apple cider vinegar

I tablespoon finely chopped peeled ginger

MAKES ABOUT ⅔ CUP

1. Stir all the ingredients together in a small saucepan and bring to a boil over medium heat. Boil, stirring occasionally, until the sauce is reduced by about half and thick enough to lightly coat a spoon, about 10 minutes. Cool before using. The glaze will keep in the refrigerator for up to three weeks.

2. Baste the ribs several times as they roast or grill using about half the sauce. Pass the remaining sauce separately.

. . . Maple Mustard Glaze

MAKES ABOUT 3/4 CUP

I know that using the liquid from bottled hot peppers sounds a little weird, but it gives this glaze a kick (from the hot peppers) and some zing (from the vinegar). It is a favorite little trick of mine that I use in all kinds of marinades, dressings, and other dishes, from salsa to tuna salad.

½ cup grainy mustard

¼ cup pure maple syrup

3 to 4 teaspoons liquid from bottled hot peppers or pickles, or hot pepper sauce to taste

Stir all the ingredients together in a small bowl. Brush the ribs lightly with the sauce several times while finishing them in the oven or on the grill, as described on page 165. Pass the remaining glaze separately.

Hot or Sweet Italian Sausages

How Many? Up to 3 pounds (about 15 links) will fit on the smoker rack at one time.

How Long? Until no trace of pink remains at the center of the sausages, about 25 minutes after closing the smoker lid.

Which Wood? Take your pick of mellow wood chips like alder and apple or more assertive woods like hickory or oak. The more heartily your sausages are seasoned and spiced, the more smoke flavor they can handle.

Cut the sausages into individual links if necessary so you can arrange them on the smoker rack with some space between each link. Poke each link in several places with a fork before smoking.

I particularly like to smoke Italian sausages—both hot and sweet—but you can smoke all kinds of uncooked sausages, including the new breed of seasoned chicken and turkey sausages turning up in supermarkets.

Pulled Pork

A North Carolina tradition, pulled pork is exactly what its name implies: slow-cooked pork, pulled by hand into shreds. Moistened with barbecue sauce—choose between the Best-of-the-Carolinas Barbecue Sauce, the Carolina-Style "Mop" Sauce, or your own personal favorite—it makes one of the best sandwiches you could ever hope to eat. Pile it high on squishy white bread or a soft-textured roll, pass coleslaw, sliced pickles, and more of the sauce for them that wants, and you're in hog heaven.

A word about the pork I use in this recipe. Typically, a whole pig or at least the whole pork shoulder (Boston butt) is the meat of choice for pulled pork. These are smoked for hours—close to a day in the case of the

One 3-pound smoked loin-end boneless pork loin roast

2 teaspoons kosher salt

2 teaspoons dry mustard

½ teaspoon paprika

¼ teaspoon cayenne pepper

2 to 2½ tablespoons hickory wood chips

Best-of-the-Carolinas Barbecue Sauce (page 19), Carolina-Style "Mop" Sauce (page 167), or 1½ cups of a barbecue sauce of your choosing

Hamburger buns or sliced white bread

Sliced sweet pickles, optional

Coleslaw (page 90), or store-bought coleslaw, optional

1. Lay the roast on your cutting board and slice it lengthwise almost completely in half, allowing you to open the roast like a book. Stir the salt, mustard, paprika, and cayenne together in a small bowl. Rub the spice mixture into all sides of the pork. Cover the pork with plastic wrap and refrigerate at least 8 hours or up to one day.

2. Make the barbecue sauce, if necessary.

3. Set up the smoker using the wood chips and smoke the pork for 45 minutes according to the directions on page 163. Use heavy-duty aluminum foil instead of the smoker lid if necessary; see page 5. When the pork has been smoking 30 minutes preheat the oven to 275°F.

4. Stir 1 cup of the barbecue sauce and ½ cup water together in a 13 × 9-inch baking dish or any baking dish large enough to hold the pork snugly. (Thinning the sauce isn't nec-

essary if you're using Carolina-Style "Mop" Sauce.) Lift the pork into the baking dish, spoon some of the liquid in the dish over the pork, and cover the dish tightly with aluminum foil. Bake until the pork is very tender and you can pull shreds from it easily, about 2 hours. Cool to room temperature.

5. Wearing rubber or latex gloves, if you like, pull the pork into shreds about ½ inch wide and 2 inches long. Return the pork to the baking dish as you work. Spoon in enough of the remaining ½ cup sauce to thoroughly moisten—but not swamp—the pork. The pork can be prepared to this point up to 2 days in advance; cover with plastic and refrigerate. Return the pulled pork to the oven until warmed through, about 30 minutes, longer for refrigerated pork. Pile the pork into a shallow bowl and serve with hamburger buns, passing the pickles and coleslaw separately if you like.

whole pig—in specially built and maintained barbecue pits. Adapting this recipe to a stovetop smoker, I found that the loin end of a pork loin roast, which is more marbled (fattier) than the rest, works beautifully.

MAKES ABOUT 8 SANDWICHES

Garlic-Studded Loin of Pork

Modern pork is very lean, which is good for your calorie count but bad for flavor. Smoking pork helps keep it moist; brining it first will help more. The pork you buy affects the final results, too. Search out a cut with a layer of fat that covers at least one side of the roast. (You can trim the fat off after smoking if you like.) And pick the most marbled cut you can find, one with visible, small streaks of fat through the eye of the meat.

MAKES 8 SERVINGS

1 bunch rosemary

½ cup plus 2 tablespoons kosher salt

2 tablespoons to ¼ cup sugar, optional

¼ cup juniper berries, optional

One 4-pound center-cut, boneless smoked loin of pork roast

1 tablespoon olive oil

½ teaspoon freshly ground black pepper

10 cloves garlic, peeled and sliced thinly

1. Pull off ¼ cup of rosemary leaves and set them aside. Heat 3 quarts water, the salt and sugar, if using, to simmering in a pot large enough to hold the liquid and pork comfortably (about 8 quarts). Stir until the sugar is dissolved, add the remaining rosemary on the branch and the juniper berries, if using, and remove the pot from the heat. Cool to room temperature.

2. Check the pork roast and, if necessary, trim off any more than ½ inch of covering fat. Submerge the pork in the brine and refrigerate 12 hours. If you like, set the pot of brine on the refrigerator shelf and add the pork to it there.

3. Finely chop the reserved rosemary leaves and stir them together with the olive oil and pepper in a small bowl. Refrigerate until needed.

4. Drain the pork thoroughly and pat it dry with paper towels. With the tip of a small knife, poke 1-inch deep slits about 2 inches apart over the entire surface of the meat. Stick one of the garlic slices into each slit. It's fine if the tops of the

garlic slices stick out a bit from the roast. Rub the rosemary paste onto the top and sides of the roast.

5. Set up the smoker using the wood chips and smoke the pork for 30 minutes, using heavy-duty aluminum foil instead of the cover according to the directions on page 5. About 20 minutes into the smoking time, position the oven rack in the center position and preheat the oven to 400°F.

6. Uncover the smoker, put the pork in the oven, and roast until an instant-read thermometer inserted into the thickest part of the roast registers 145°F, about 20 minutes. Let the pork rest 10 to 20 minutes.

7. Carve the pork into ½-inch slices and serve warm.

Prune-Stuffed Loin Pork Chops

If you make a pocket in the chops with as narrow an opening as possible, the stuffing will stay put and not ooze out during smoking. This little bit of information and a small, heavy-strength plastic bag to get the stuffing into the pocket are all you need for a moist, plump chop filled with sweet and fragrant prune stuffing. These are wonderful served with buttered parsnips, fluffy mashed potatoes, or thickish rounds of new potatoes seasoned with olive oil, salt, and pepper and roasted until crispy and deep golden brown.

MAKES 4 SERVINGS

3 tablespoons unsalted butter

1 small Spanish onion, diced very fine (about ½ cup)

½ cup finely chopped dried pitted prunes

3 tablespoons Cognac or brandy

Kosher salt

Freshly ground black pepper

4 thick (about 1¼ inches) smoked loin pork chops

1½ tablespoons hickory wood chips

1. Heat the butter in a small skillet over medium heat. Add the onions and cook, stirring occasionally, until golden brown, about 8 minutes. Stir in the prunes and cook until heated through, 1 to 2 minutes. Pour in the Cognac and bring to a boil. Adjust the heat so the liquid is simmering and cook until the liquid is gone. Season generously with salt and pepper and cool to room temperature.

2. Prepare the chops for stuffing: If you look at the chops, you will see an L-shaped bone and a rounded edge of pork that runs between them. Pick a spot on the edge of the meat about halfway between the bones. Insert the tip of a paring knife into the eye of the chop. Keeping the blade parallel to the work surface, start to cut a pocket in the eye of the chop while enlarging the opening of the pocket as little as possible. Turn the sharp part of the knife blade in the other direction to complete the pocket. Be careful not to extend the pocket to more than within ½ inch of the sides of the chop.

3. Scrape the stuffing into a 1-quart heavy-strength resealable bag and press it into one corner of the bag. Cut about ¼ inch from the corner of the bag with the filling in it and insert the cut tip as far as possible into the opening of one of the chops. With gentle steady pressure, squeeze about one-

fourth of the stuffing into the chop. Repeat with the remaining chops. If any stuffing oozes out of the chops while you are filling them, simply scrape it back into the bag. Massage the stuffing away from the opening and toward the bones, then seal the opening with two toothpicks in an X pattern. Rub the chops with a generous amount of salt and pepper.

4. Set up the smoker using the wood chips and smoke the chops according to the directions on page 162 until an instant-read thermometer inserted into the thickest part of the chop near the bone registers 145°F, about 25 minutes. Remove and let stand 5 minutes before serving.

Apple-Cured Pork Tenderloin with Sweet and Sour Cabbage

I like to back up the flavor in a finished dish with a reinforcing or complementary flavor note, as I do in the Ultimate Corn Bread (page 229) or Triple Mushroom Beef Tenderloin Steaks (page 204). Here, I use apple juice in place of part of the water in the seasoning brine, then sauté apples and cabbage together for a side dish. The combination works beautifully.

MAKES 6 SERVINGS

1 quart apple juice

¼ cup plus 2 tablespoons kosher salt, plus more for seasoning the cabbage

¼ cup whole allspice berries

2 tablespoons black peppercorns

Two whole smoked pork tenderloins (about 2 pounds)

2 Gala or Fuji apples

2 tablespoons vegetable oil

1 small (about 2-pound) head red cabbage, quartered, core removed, and leaves cut into ¼-inch strips

¼ cup white wine vinegar

1½ tablespoons oak or maple wood chips

1 tablespoon sugar, optional

Freshly ground black pepper

1. Bring the apple juice, 1 quart water, and the salt to a boil in a large saucepan over medium heat. Stir in the allspice and peppercorns. Cool the brine to room temperature.

2. Meanwhile, trim the pork tenderloins according to the directions on page 163. When the brine is cool, slip in the pork tenderloins and refrigerate 6 to 8 hours. The tenderloins can be brined the day before you plan to serve them. Drain them thoroughly, pat them dry, and store them wrapped in plastic wrap in the refrigerator.

3. Cut the apples in quarters through the core. Cut out the core section from each quarter, then peel the apples. Cut the apple pieces crosswise into ¼-inch slices.

4. Heat the oil in a large deep skillet over medium heat. Stir in the apples and cook, stirring occasionally, until lightly browned, about 8 minutes. Meanwhile, separate the cabbage leaves as much as possible.

5. Scatter the cabbage into the pan and season lightly with salt. Stir until they are glossy and slightly wilted, about

4 minutes. Pour in 3 tablespoons of the vinegar, reduce the heat to low, and cover the pan. Cook until the thickest parts of the cabbage leaves are tender but still firm, about 30 minutes. Stir the cabbage occasionally as it cooks and check to make sure there is a small amount of liquid in the pan. If all the liquid evaporates and the cabbage begins to stick, add a tablespoon or two of water. The cabbage may be prepared to this point up to 2 hours in advance.

6. Set up the smoker using the wood chips and smoke the tenderloins according to the directions on page 163 until an instant-read thermometer inserted into the thickest part of the pork registers 145°F, about 25 minutes.

7. While the pork is smoking, finish the cabbage: Stir in the remaining 1 tablespoon vinegar, then taste the cabbage. If you would like it a little sweeter, add the sugar. Heat the cabbage over medium heat, stirring frequently, until all the liquid is evaporated and the cabbage begins to brown, about 10 minutes. Season with salt and pepper and cover the skillet to keep the cabbage warm.

8. Remove the pork to a carving board and let stand 5 minutes. Carve the pork into ½-inch slices and arrange a few overlapping slices on a serving plate. Flank the pork with the sautéed cabbage and apples. Serve warm.

Country-Style Pork and White Bean Casserole

The wonderful thing about slow-cooked dishes like this one is the give-and-take between ingredients. Here, the beans absorb the smokiness of the pork and the pork takes on the flavor of rosemary and the aroma of the vegetables. A word of warning: a Dutch oven full of pork and beans makes a hefty handful to lift hot from the oven. Make sure you have thick, dry pot holders and a safe place close to the oven to put the pot down. Also, get help if you need it.

MAKES 8 SERVINGS

I pound dried small white beans, such as navy beans, great Northern beans, or baby limas

One 3-pound smoked boneless pork shoulder roast

Kosher salt

Freshly ground black pepper

2 tablespoons apple, cherry, or alder wood chips

3 tablespoons olive oil, plus more for serving

2 medium onions, cut into large dice (about 2½ cups)

2 medium carrots, peeled and cut into large dice (about I cup)

2 celery stalks, trimmed and cut into large dice (about I cup)

One 46-ounce can reduced-sodium chicken broth

One 15-ounce can diced tomatoes and their liquid

2 sprigs fresh rosemary

2 bay leaves

Pesto (page 63), optional

1. Pour enough water over the beans in a deep bowl to cover them by 4 inches. Soak the beans at room temperature for 6 hours or in the refrigerator for 12 to 24 hours.

2. Trim all but a thin layer of fat from the pork roast, if necessary. Tie lengths of kitchen twine around the roast at 1½-inch intervals. (This will make the roast easier to lift from the casserole and onto a carving board once it is cooked.) Rub a generous amount of salt and pepper into the roast. Set up the smoker using the wood chips and heavy-duty aluminum foil instead of the cover and smoke the pork according to the directions on page 4 for 45 minutes. The pork will still be quite pink at the center; it will finish cooking in the oven.

3. While the pork is smoking, prepare the beans. Preheat the oven to 300°F with the rack in the center position. Heat 3

tablespoons olive oil in an 8-quart Dutch oven or heavy pot over medium heat. Add the onions, carrots, and celery and stir occasionally until they are lightly browned, about 8 minutes.

4. Pour in the chicken broth. Drain the beans and add them to the pot along with the tomatoes, rosemary, and bay leaves. Bring to a boil, then adjust the heat to a simmer.

5. When the pork is done smoking, slip it into the beans and set the casserole on the oven rack. Bake until the beans are tender and the pork is fork tender, about 3 hours. By the time the pork is tender there should be just enough of a syrupy liquid left to coat the beans generously. If the beans are swimming in liquid, see the instructions at the end of the next step.

6. Set a carving board next to the casserole and slip two kitchen forks or large spoons under a length of twine on either end of the roast. Lift the pork gently from the beans, let it drip a second or two over the pot, and place on the board. If there is more than just enough liquid to coat the beans, place the casserole over medium heat and bring the liquid to a boil. Cook, stirring, until the liquid is thickened and reduced slightly and there is just enough of it to generously coat the beans. Let the beans and pork rest 10 minutes.

7. Carve thick slices of the pork and serve them over the beans in warm shallow soup bowls. Pass olive oil and pesto, if using, separately.

OPTIONAL CRUNCHY TOPPING

¾ cup coarse dry breadcrumbs

¼ cup grated Parmesan cheese

2 tablespoons melted unsalted butter or olive oil

If you'd like to finish the casserole with this topping, increase the oven temperature to 425°F after removing the pork to a carving board. Stir the breadcrumbs, Parmesan, and butter together in a small bowl. Sprinkle the crumb mixture over the beans and return the casserole to the oven. Bake until crunchy and golden brown, about 10 minutes. Tent the pork with aluminum foil to keep it warm while the topping is browning.

Smoked Pork Medallions with Shameless Succotash

Four 6-ounce smoked boneless pork loin chops

Kosher salt

Freshly ground black pepper

1½ tablespoons apple wood chips or other mild-flavored wood chips such as alder or cherry

2 tablespoons unsalted butter

One 10-ounce box frozen lima beans, defrosted

3 scallions, trimmed and thinly sliced, green and white parts separated

One 10-ounce box frozen corn, defrosted

¼ cup light cream or half-and-half

¼ cup homemade or canned reduced-sodium chicken broth

Succotash used to be dead-of-winter food, made by Native Americans and early colonists with lima beans and corn that were dried after harvest. You can make a much springier version with frozen baby limas and corn. No need to feel like you're cheating—both vegetables are wonderful frozen and make an excellent side dish for the sweet flavor of smoked pork. I keep a box or two of each on hand for quickie meals like this one.

MAKES 4 SERVINGS

1. Rub both sides of the pork chops generously with salt and pepper. Set up the smoker using the wood chips and smoke the pork according to the directions on page 162 until an instant-read thermometer inserted into the thickest part of the pork registers 145°F, about 22 minutes. If the pork is done smoking before the vegetables in the next step are ready, remove the pork to a plate and set aside.

2. While the pork is smoking, melt the butter in a heavy large skillet over medium-low heat. Add the lima beans and white parts of the scallions and season them lightly with salt and pepper. Cover the pan and cook until the limas are heated through, about 6 minutes. Stir in the corn, cover, and cook until both vegetables are tender but not mushy, about 8 minutes.

3. Uncover the pan, pour in the cream and broth, and bring to a boil. Boil until the liquid is reduced by two-thirds. Stir in the green parts of the scallions and tuck the pork into the succotash. Turn the pieces to coat them lightly with sauce and rewarm them, if necessary. Serve hot on warm plates, spooning the succotash over and around the pork medallions.

Smoked Italian Sausage and Peppers

These macho sausages make unbelievably good sandwiches or an unbeatable cold weather main course, alongside mashed or roasted potatoes. Or, pluck the sausages out of the sauce and use the sauce to dress a pound of rigatoni. Serve the sausages on the side and pass plenty of grated Parmesan or Romano cheese.

MAKES 4 SERVINGS

2 pounds smoked hot or sweet Italian sausages, (page 169), or a mix of the two

3 tablespoons olive oil

4 garlic cloves, thinly sliced

2 large yellow onions, cut in half, then into ½-inch strips (about 3 cups)

2 large red or green bell peppers, cored, seeded, and cut into ½-inch strips (about 3 cups)

½ pound cremini or white mushrooms, sliced (about 2½ cups), optional

Kosher salt

Freshly ground black pepper

2 tablespoons tomato paste

2 teaspoons dried oregano, optional

½ cup dry red wine

2 cups homemade or canned reduced-sodium chicken broth

1. Smoke the sausages according to the directions on page 169. The sausages may be smoked up to 1 day in advance, wrapped in plastic, and stored in the refrigerator.

2. While the sausages are smoking, heat the olive oil in a large (at least 12 inches), deep skillet or casserole over medium-high heat. Add the garlic and cook, shaking the pan, just until it begins to brown. Scatter the onions and peppers into the pan and cook, stirring, until they are wilted, about 8 minutes. Stir in the mushrooms, if using them. Adjust the heat to medium-low, season the vegetables lightly with salt and pepper, and cook, stirring often, until the onions and peppers are tender, about 15 minutes.

3. Increase the heat to high and cook until the vegetables begin to sizzle, about 3 minutes. Stir in the tomato paste and oregano and cook, stirring, 2 minutes. Pour in the wine and bring to a boil. Cook until the wine is almost completely evaporated, then pour in the chicken broth and tuck the sausages into the vegetables. Adjust the heat so the liquid is boiling gently and cook until there is just enough liquid to lightly coat the sausages and vegetables, about 12 minutes. The sausages and peppers may be prepared completely up to 2 days in advance. Add about ½ cup chicken broth or water and reheat over medium-low heat until the sausages are heated through before serving.

beef

and

lamb

Beef Brisket

Finding a whole beef brisket in a supermarket or butcher shop is a rarity. Most commonly, briskets sold at retail markets are cut into two parts, known as the point cut and the flat cut. The point cut is fattier, and therefore more flavorful than the flat cut; both are tough cuts that benefit from slow cooking with some kind of liquid. You make the call, but when I smoke brisket, it's always the point cut. If you are concerned about fat, you can always trim much of it after cooking. But remember that while the brisket smokes and slow-cooks in the oven, the fat will keep it moister.

The method outlined here smokes the brisket first to infuse it with flavor, then finishes it off in the oven, where it steams on the rack over its own juices until tender.

How Many? One flat cut or point cut brisket weighing up to 3 pounds will fit on the smoker rack.

How Long? Until the brisket is very tender when poked with a fork; on the stovetop for 45 minutes, then about 3 hours in the oven.

Which Wood? Go for the gusto with 2 tablespoons, or more, of mesquite, oak, or hickory wood chips.

Most supermarket-purchased briskets are very well trimmed, usually with no more than 1/8-inch or so of fat. If you can find one with a thicker layer of fat, get it. The fat will help keep the brisket moist during the extended smoking and baking. If you want to **trim** any from the surface of brisket, I suggest you do that after cooking.

Season a 3-pound brisket generously by rubbing 4 teaspoons kosher salt and 1 teaspoon coarsely ground black pepper into all sides. If you can do this a full day in advance of smoking, so much the better. Wrap the beef in plastic wrap and refrigerate until half an hour before you begin smoking. Alternatively, brine a 3-pound brisket (see page 11) for 5 to 7 hours.

Start the brisket on the rack fat side up (if there is one). Even if it appears you can close the smoker lid with the brisket on the rack, tent the smoker with aluminum foil (see page 5) instead of using the lid. During cooking the brisket will shrink in length and expand in the center. Getting the smoker lid off may not be as easy as getting it on.

Combo-Cooking: After the brisket has been smoking for 30 minutes, preheat the oven to 275°F with the rack in the center position. When the brisket is done smoking, slide the smoker, with the brisket still covered, into the oven and bake until done as described above.

Check the brisket after it has been in the oven 3 hours. The safest and most accurate way to do this is to remove the smoking pan to the stove top, then close the oven door. With a protected hand, peel back a corner of the aluminum foil and let the steam escape. Uncover just enough of the foil to allow you to check the tenderness with a fork. If the brisket requires more cooking, carefully reseal the pan and return it to the oven.

Serve the brisket hot, sliced thin with piles of mashed potatoes into which you've folded some golden brown sautéed onion. Or serve it room temperature with coleslaw and/or potato salad. Leftover brisket, sliced thin and piled onto an onion roll and topped with any kind of coleslaw you like, is a beautiful thing.

Flank Steak

Like the skirt steak on page 193, I recommend you smoke a flank steak as a way to flavor it before either grilling or broiling it. Also like the skirt steak, a flank steak can be smoked a day or two in advance and popped on the grill or under the broiler to finish it off.

How Many? One 1½ to 1¾-pound flank steak will fit on the smoker rack.

How Long? If you plan to finish the steak on the grill or under the broiler, as described in Combo-Cooking, smoke it until an instant-read thermometer inserted into the thickest part of the steak registers 115°F (very rare); about 20 minutes after closing the smoker lid. If you choose not to broil or grill the steak after smoking it, a 1½-pound flank steak will cook to medium-rare (130°F) in about 25 minutes; smoke a few minutes longer for a medium steak.

Which Wood? Flank steak can stand up to assertive woods, like 1½ tablespoons of mesquite or hickory, or 2 tablespoons of bourbon-soaked oak.

Season the flank by rubbing 1½ teaspoons kosher salt and ½ teaspoon freshly ground black pepper into both sides. The seasonings will penetrate the beef more thoroughly if you rub the flank and refrigerate it a day ahead of smoking.

Combo-Cooking: Smoking the average (1½-pound) flank steak for 20 to 22 minutes will render a very rare center (about 115°F). Remove the flank from the smoker immediately after it reaches this temperature and cool it to room temperature. Finish the steak on a gas or charcoal grill or under the broiler, to any degree of doneness from rare to well-done: with your grill set 4 inches above the coals, or a broiler pan about 4 inches under the broiler, a room temperature smoked flank steak will take about 2½ minutes per side to cook to rare; 3½ minutes per side to reach medium-rare and 4 minutes per side to reach medium. You may also refrigerate a smoked flank steak for up to two days before grilling or broiling it. Allow a minute or so longer of cooking on each side for a refrigerated steak.

Serve the steak sliced thinly against the grain (crosswise) with **Spicy-Cool Avocado Sauce** (page 16) or **Smoked Tomatillo Sauce** (page 15) if you like. Sliced tomatoes seasoned with coarse salt, freshly ground black pepper, and a fruity olive oil make a nice accompaniment. So does a Caesar or mixed green salad.

Tenderloin Steaks

There are times when finishing a cut of smoked meat on a grill or under a broiler really sends it over the top, as is the case with skirt steak (page 193) or baby back ribs (page 165). I expected that to be the case with tenderloin steaks, but they were absolutely delicious right out of the smoker. You can, however, finish them off in a hot pan as described here to crisp up the surfaces.

How Many? Up to six 7 to 8-ounce tenderloin steaks will fit on the smoker rack at one time. It is easier to cook thick— about 1½-inch—fillets to rare to medium-rare. Thinner steaks, in the 1 to 1¼-inch range, will give you a smokier flavor and a more well-done center.

How Long? Until an instant-read thermometer inserted into the thickest part of the fillet registers 125°F for rare (about 20 minutes for a 1½-inch thick steak) or 130°F for medium-rare (about 22 minutes for a 1½-inch thick steak); longer, of course, for more well-done steaks. Steaks cut 1¼ inches thick will reach medium-rare in about 20 minutes; medium in about 22 minutes.

Which Wood? Try 1½ tablespoons of hickory, mesquite, or oak wood chips for a mellow flavor. Up the amount to 2 tablespoons for a heartier flavor.

Trim any excess fat from the sides of the steaks (not usually an issue with tenderloin).

Season each fillet steak with a scant ½ teaspoon kosher salt and two generous pinches of freshly ground black pepper and rub the seasoning into the steak.

Check the fillets for doneness with an instant-read thermometer after 20 minutes.

Combo-Cooking: If you like, crisp the outside of the steaks after smoking: coat the bottom of a heavy, nonstick, or cast iron pan large enough to hold the steak(s) comfortably with a thin coat of olive oil. Heat the pan over medium-high heat about 2 minutes before the steaks are done smoking. Lift the steaks into the pan with tongs and cook, turning once, until browned on both sides, about 1 minute per side.

Serve the steaks as is, right out of the smoker or pan. If you like steak sauce, pass it around. Fillet steaks are a dressy entrée. Accessorize them with roasted asparagus spears or roasted halved plum tomatoes topped with Parmesan breadcrumbs.

Strip or Sirloin Steaks

How Many? Up to four 10-ounce, 1¼-inch thick steaks will fit on the smoker rack at one time.

How Long? For a medium-rare steak, until an instant-read thermometer inserted into the thickest part of the steak registers 125°F; for a steak of the above-mentioned size, about 16 minutes, longer for a thicker or more well-done steak. If you plan to finish your steak on a grill or in a grill pan (see Combo-Cooking), remove them from the smoker after 14 minutes.

Which Wood? Start with 2 tablespoons bourbon-soaked oak or maple wood chips for a mellower flavor; 2½ tablespoons mesquite or hickory wood chips for more of a kick.

Trim any fat in excess of ¼ inch from the edges of the steaks.

Season each steak with 1 teaspoon kosher salt and ¼ teaspoon coarsely ground black pepper, rubbing it into the steak several hours before smoking if possible. Or rub 1 teaspoon of the **Mushroom-Herb Rub** (page 27) into the steak an hour or so before smoking.

Check the steaks for doneness with an instant-read thermometer after they have been smoking for 15 minutes.

Combo-Cooking: For a crisp exterior, pull the steaks from the smoker two minutes before the time suggested above. Finish the steaks in a hot heavy skillet or over hot coals according to the directions under Combo-Cooking in the following recipe. Strip or sirloin steaks are best grilled or pan-fried shortly after smoking—without refrigeration.

Skirt Steak

How Many? One 1 to 1½-pound skirt steak, cut in half crosswise will fit on the smoker rack.

How Long? You will have to cut a whole skirt steak in half crosswise for it to fit in the smoker. One end of the steak will be considerably thinner and cook faster than the other half. If you would like to cook both halves to the same doneness, add the thinner piece to the smoker after the thicker piece has been smoking for about 8 minutes. If you are not planning to finish the steak as described in Combo-Cooking, smoke the halves until an instant-read thermometer inserted into the thickest part of each half registers 125°F for a medium-rare steak, about 24 minutes after closing the smoker lid, longer for more well done steaks. (Skirt steaks are a little tricky to check for doneness with an instant-read thermometer. Poke the thickest part of the steak with the thermometer in a few places, aiming for the center of the steak.) If you do plan to grill the steak after smoking, cook the steaks to a temperature of 100 to 105°F, which will take about 18 minutes. The steaks can be smoked up to 2 days before grilling them.

Which Wood? The striated texture of skirt steak means it will soak up smoke like a sponge, so take it a mite easy: 1 to 1½ tablespoons of hickory or oak wood chips, or 1½ to 2 tablespoons of a mellower wood like alder.

Trim any excess fat from the surface of the steak and cut the steak in half crosswise.

Season skirt steak with a generous rubbing of kosher salt and freshly ground black pepper or 2 teaspoons **Southwestern Rub** (page 28).

Combo-Cooking: Skirt steaks benefit greatly from a short trip to a gas or charcoal grill, or a preheated ridged grill

This is one of those good news/bad news scenarios. I'll give you the bad news first: skirt steak, as it emerges from the smoker, does not have the most wonderful texture. Now for the good news: if you use smoking as a way to season a skirt steak before you grill or pan-fry it, you will be rewarded with the best-tasting skirt steak you ever tucked in to, or turned into a fajita (page 197). Now for the very good news: you can do the smoking part a day or two in advance, leaving the final few minutes of cooking for the main event.

Most likely you will be buying a whole skirt steak. You'll have to cut it in two so it fits in the smoker. Skirt steaks vary in thickness from one end to the other.

pan, after smoking. If you've smoked them for 12 to 15 minutes as described above, and grill them cold from the refrigerator, you will have a medium-rare steak by the time the outside is browned and crispy, about 4 minutes. Cook longer for more well-done steaks.

Serve smoked skirt steaks hot from the smoker or grill with **Fresh Tomato Salsa** (page 22), either alone or spooned onto a baked potato. **Spicy-Cool Avocado Sauce** (page 16) is also a nice way to go. Smoked skirt steak is delicious in **My Favorite Fajitas** (page 197).

Hamburgers

How Many? Up to six 6-ounce burgers will fit on the smoker rack at one time.

How Long? Until an instant-read thermometer inserted into the center of the burger registers 125°F (for a medium-rare burger); about 16 minutes after closing the smoker lid for a 6-ounce, 1-inch-thick burger; slightly longer for more well-done or larger hamburgers. If you plan to sear your burgers in a pan after smoking them (see Combo-Cooking), remove them at about 14 minutes.

Which Wood? 2 to 2½ tablespoons of hickory or mesquite wood chips.

Season the beef for burgers before you smoke them: crumble the beef into a wide bowl. For each ¾ pound (two hamburgers' worth) of ground beef, sprinkle 1¼ teaspoons kosher salt or less to taste and ½ teaspoon freshly ground black pepper over the beef. Work the seasoning gently into the meat and form into 1-inch-thick patties. (See the box for more seasoning suggestions.)

Check the hamburgers for doneness with an instant-read thermometer after 15 minutes.

Combo-Cooking: For burgers with a crusty-brown outside, finish them off in a hot skillet: when the burgers have been smoking 12 minutes, heat a lightly oiled heavy nonstick or cast iron pan over medium-high heat. Lift the burgers with a spatula from the smoker to the pan and cook long enough just to crisp the outer surface, about 1 minute per side.

QUICKIE BURGER SEASONINGS

Instead of the salt and pepper, season each 12 ounces of ground beef with either of the following. Stir the seasonings together in a small bowl, then sprinkle them over ground beef crumbled into a bowl.

4 teaspoons Worcestershire sauce

4 teaspoons mustard

1 teaspoon kosher salt

½ teaspoon freshly ground black pepper

OR

1 tablespoon soy sauce

1 teaspoon ground cumin

½ teaspoon kosher salt

Lamb Chops

You can smoke any kind of lamb chop you like: largish, blade chops from near the shoulder that are streaked with fat; meatier rib chops with their lollipop shape; or my favorites— the smallish loin chops that resemble miniature T-bone steaks. In any case, choose chops that are about 1¼ inches thick and season them well with kosher salt and black pepper as far in advance of smoking as possible.

How Many? Up to 8 (about 1 pound) loin or rib chops or 4 shoulder chops will fit on the smoker rack at one time.

How Long? Until an instant-read thermometer inserted in the thickest part of the chop next to a bone registers 130°F (for medium-rare); about 20 minutes after closing the smoker lid for rib or loin chops, 25 to 30 minutes for shoulder chops.

Which Wood? I prefer milder woods like 2 tablespoons of apple or alder chips, with lamb. You may find an equal amount of more assertive wood chips like hickory or oak work for you.

Trim any excess fat from the sides of the chops.

Season rib or loin chops with a generous ¼ teaspoon kosher salt and a healthy pinch of freshly ground black pepper each; double that amount for shoulder chops. Rub the seasonings into the lamb and let them stand at room temperature for 30 minutes or, preferably, refrigerate them for at least 4 hours or up to 24 hours.

Check the chops for doneness with an instant-read thermometer after they have been smoking 16 minutes (rib or loin chops) or 20 minutes (shoulder chops).

Combo-Cooking: If you like, crisp up the chops after smoking. Heat a lightly oiled heavy nonstick or cast iron pan large enough to hold the chops comfortably over medium-high heat about 2 minutes before the chops are done smoking. Transfer the chops to the pan with tongs and cook, turning once, until browned on both sides, about 1 minute per side.

Serve smoked lamb chops with buttered peas and roasted potatoes, passing grainy mustard around the table separately. Or take them in another direction altogether and serve with the **Cranberry Relish** on page 24 and a big bowl of couscous flavored with toasted walnuts and cinnamon.

My Favorite Fajitas

1 large smoked skirt steak
(about ½ pounds)

FOR THE MARINADE

2 teaspoons cumin seeds

2 limes

3 garlic cloves, peeled and
sliced

1 teaspoon kosher salt

1 teaspoon crushed red pepper
flakes

FOR THE ACCOMPANIMENTS

3 tablespoons vegetable oil

2 large red onions, peeled,
cut in half and then into
¼-inch strips

2 large green bell peppers,
cored, seeded, and cut
into ¼-inch strips

2 large red bell peppers,
cored, seeded, and cut
into ¼-inch strips

Kosher salt

8 flour tortillas

Smoky-Spicy Salsa (page 21)
or your own favorite
homemade or store-
bought salsa

Sour cream

It's the little things . . . In this case, the little things are toasted cumin seeds that add zip to the marinade and a preliminary smoking that adds character to a grilled skirt steak.

MAKES 4 SERVINGS

1. Smoke the skirt steak according to the directions on page 193 to an internal temperature of 105 to 110°F, about 15 minutes.

2. Make the marinade: while the steak is cooling, toast the cumin seeds in a small skillet over medium-low heat, shaking them constantly so they don't burn or stick, just until they are fragrant, about 3 minutes. Let them cool. Squeeze the juice from the limes into a 1-gallon heavy plastic resealable bag. Add the cumin seeds, garlic, 1 teaspoon salt, and the pepper flakes and swish the marinade around to dissolve the salt. Slip the cooled steaks into the marinade, press out most of the air

from the bag, and seal the bag very tightly. Refrigerate the beef for at least 4 hours or up to 1 day, turning the bag several times.

3. To prepare the accompaniments, heat the vegetable oil in a large, deep skillet over medium heat. Stir in the red onions and cook, stirring often, until they are wilted, about 5 minutes. Add the green peppers and cook until they are wilted enough to make room for the red peppers. Add the red peppers, season the vegetables lightly with salt, and adjust the heat to low. Cook, stirring often, until tender, about 20 minutes. The vegetables can be prepared several hours in advance. Reheat them over low heat just before serving.

To prepare the fajitas indoors: Preheat the oven to 350°F. Wrap the tortillas in aluminum foil. Reheat the vegetables if necessary. Drain the steak well and discard the marinade. Heat a lightly oiled large grill pan or heavy skillet over medium-high heat until smoking. Cook the steak, turning once, just until seared on both sides, about 5 minutes. At this point the steak will be about medium-rare. Turn off the heat and continue cooking in the hot pan for a more well-done steak. Remove the steak from the skillet to a carving board and let it rest about 5 minutes. Pop the tortillas into the oven and let them warm while the steak is resting.

To prepare the fajitas on a charcoal or gas grill: Wrap the tortillas in aluminum foil. Reheat the vegetables if necessary, using a corner of the grill if there is room. Drain the steak well and discard the marinade. Cook the steak on the hottest part of the grill until both sides are well browned, about 6 minutes. The steak at this point will be about medium-rare; move the steak to a cooler part of the grill and continue to cook it for a more well-done steak. Remove the steak to a carving board and let it rest about 5 minutes. Set the tortillas on a moderately hot part of the grill and let them warm, turning once or twice, while the steak rests.

To serve: Cut the steak crosswise into thin slices and pile the slices on a serving plate. Serve the vegetables directly from the skillet or scoop them into a serving bowl. Pass the tortillas, salsa, sour cream, steak, and vegetables around the table and let everyone dress their own fajitas as they like.

Margaritas

Margaritas match beautifully with fajitas and are a foolproof way to break the ice at a backyard barbecue. Designate one person as bartender (there's at least one natural-born mixologist in every crowd) or mix the first for your guests and let them help themselves to refills. Cocktail shakers are inexpensive, widely available, and absolutely necessary for chilled, frothy cocktails.

Talking tequila with real aficionados is like striking up a conversation with a cigar nut about what's in his humidor lately—be prepared to pull up a chair. Tequila, once thought of as something to do between licking the salt and sucking the lemon, has come a long way, and there are many varieties to choose from.

2 cups (16 ounces) good-quality tequila

1 cup (8 ounces) Cointreau, good quality curaçao, or other orange liqueur

½ cup fresh lime juice

Kosher salt

Lime wedges

Coarsely cracked ice

Stir the tequila, Cointreau, and lime juice together in a small pitcher. Cover with plastic wrap and chill until needed, up to one day. Just before serving, spread an even layer of kosher salt on a small plate. Rub the rims of 5-ounce cocktail glasses, or small, straight-sided highball glasses, with a wedge of lime and dip them in the salt. Set up a bar area, keeping the pitcher, cocktail shaker, bucket of cracked ice, and glasses close together.

For two margaritas: Fill the metal part of a cocktail shaker about two-thirds with cracked ice. Pour in about ¾ cup of the margarita mix. Cap with the glass part of the shaker and tap gently to make sure it is firmly seated. Holding the glass and metal parts of the shaker parallel to the floor and clasped tightly together, shake the margarita vigorously until very frothy and ice cold. When you think you have shaken it enough, shake it another 5 to 10 seconds. Set the metal part flat on a table and lift off the glass, holding the metal cup firmly and giving the glass a good sideways rap, if necessary, to free it. Fit the cocktail strainer over the metal cup and strain into the prepared glasses. Serve immediately. If you don't have a cocktail shaker and strainer, stir the margarita mix and ice together vigorously for a minute or so in a tall glass with an iced tea spoon or regular spoon until very well chilled. Then pour the margarita into the prepared glasses, holding the ice back with the spoon.

You might want to invest a little more in a reposado, or "rested" tequila—one that has been aged in wood for two to twelve months. I prefer the clean, bright flavor of Cointreau for margaritas, but it is a little pricey. If you can find a good, not-too-sweet curaçao, that will do fine. I try to avoid triple sec—I find it too sweet. But if you and your guests like a slightly sweeter drink, then by all means go with it.

MAKES EIGHT 4-OUNCE DRINKS (CAN BE EASILY DOUBLED OR HALVED)

Barbecued Short Ribs of Beef

Throughout the book, I suggest you smoke certain cuts of meat or poultry before finishing them off by roasting, grilling, or broiling them. Here, Combo-Cooking works in reverse: tough short ribs of beef are simmered slowly in barbecue sauce to tenderize and flavor them before they are smoked. In most cases, when a recipe calls for Combo-Cooking, some of the steps can be done well in advance. These ribs are no exception. Bake the ribs up to three days before you plan to serve them. A quick trip to the smoker will both heat the ribs up and imbue them with a smoky flavor.

MAKES 4 SERVINGS

8 pieces (about 2 × 2 inches each) meaty smoked beef short ribs (about 3 pounds)

Kosher salt

Freshly ground black pepper

3 tablespoons vegetable oil

1 cup beer or water

Barbecue Sauce (page 18) or 2 cups of your favorite barbecue sauce

2 tablespoons hickory, oak, or mesquite wood chips

1. Rub all sides of the short ribs generously with salt and pepper. Heat the oil in a large Dutch oven or heavy pot over medium heat. Add as many of the short ribs as will fit comfortably and cook, turning as necessary, until they are well browned on all sides, about 10 minutes. Adjust the heat if necessary so the beef browns and cooks evenly without splattering. Drain the short ribs on paper towels and, if necessary, brown the remaining pieces.

2. Pour or spoon off all the fat from the pan. Return the Dutch oven to the heat, pour in the beer and bring to a boil, scraping the brown bits from the bottom of the pot. Boil until the liquid is reduced by about half. Stir in the barbecue sauce, tuck the pieces of beef into the sauce, and bring to a boil. Adjust the heat so the liquid is simmering. Cover the pot and cook, turning the pieces in the sauce a few times, until the beef is tender when poked with a fork, about 2½ hours.

3. Cool the beef in the liquid, then remove the short rib pieces to a plate, scraping as much sauce from the ribs back into the pot as you can. Cover the ribs with plastic wrap and refrigerate. Scrape the sauce into a small saucepan and refrigerate. When the sauce is chilled, remove the solidified fat from the surface. The beef and sauce can be prepared to this point up to three days in advance.

4. To serve the beef: Set up the smoker using the wood chips and smoke the beef as described on page 4 until the beef is heated through, about 30 minutes.

5. Reheat the sauce over low heat to simmering. Transfer the short ribs to a warm platter and spoon the sauce over them. Serve immediately.

Triple Mushroom Beef Tenderloin Steaks

Seasoning the fillets with Mushroom-Herb Rub and serving them with a mix of mushrooms spiked with spirits gives these steaks an injection of mushroom flavor.

MAKES 4 SERVINGS

Four 8-ounce beef tenderloin steaks, each about 1¼ inches thick

4 teaspoons Mushroom-Herb Rub (page 27)

2 tablespoons olive oil

2 tablespoons unsalted butter

1 leek, white and light green part only, cleaned (see page 61) and sliced ½ inch (about 2 cups)

3 garlic cloves, minced

Kosher salt

8 ounces white or cremini mushrooms, cleaned and trimmed, cut into ¼-inch slices

4 ounces shiitake mushrooms, cleaned, stems removed, caps sliced ¼ inch

4 ounces oyster mushrooms

Freshly ground black pepper

2 tablespoons cherry, oak, or bourbon-soaked oak wood chips

1. Season each of the steaks with 1 teaspoon of the rub, rubbing it into both sides of the steak. Cover the steaks and let them stand at room temperature 30 minutes or, preferably, refrigerate them for up to one day.

2. Heat the oil and butter in a large, heavy skillet over medium heat. Add the leek and garlic, season lightly with salt, and cook, stirring, until the leek is wilted and lightly browned, about 5 minutes.

3. Stir in the white mushrooms. Cook, tossing occasionally, until they begin to soften. Stir in the shiitakes and cook, stirring, until the two mushrooms are lightly browned and tender, about 10 minutes. While they are cooking, trim the hard parts of the oyster mushrooms where the stems meet. Tear the oyster mushrooms in pieces roughly 1 inch wide. When the shiitake mushrooms are brown, add the oyster mushrooms, season lightly with salt, and cook until softened,

about 5 minutes. Remove from the heat and season to taste with salt and pepper.

4. Set up the smoker using the wood chips and smoke the steaks according to the directions on page 190 until an instant-read thermometer inserted into the thickest part of the steak registers 125°F for a medium-rare steak. Smoke longer for more well-done steaks. (See page 190 for instructions on Combo-Cooking filet steaks.) Remove and let stand 5 minutes.

5. While the steaks are resting, heat the mushrooms over low heat until hot and check the seasoning one last time. Serve each steak on a bed of the mushrooms, reserving a few mushrooms for topping each steak.

Beef, Pepper, and Red Onion Kabobs

Sautéing the onion and pepper first gives them a head start so the beef won't overcook by the time they're tender. If you serve these at a barbecue, smoke them about 5 minutes less than outlined below—up to a day in advance—and finish them off on the grill.

MAKES 4 KABOBS

1 tablespoon olive oil

1 large red onion (about 10 ounces), cut into 1½-inch squares

1 large yellow bell pepper, cored, seeded, and cut into 1½-inch squares

Kosher salt

Freshly ground black pepper

Rosemary-Garlic Rub (page 29) or Southwestern Rub (page 28), optional

1 pound trimmed beef tenderloin steak, about 1 inch thick, cut into 1-inch cubes

2 tablespoons hickory or mesquite wood chips

1. Heat the oil in a large skillet over medium heat. Add the onion and bell pepper and season them generously with salt, pepper, and rub, if using. Cook, tossing often, just until the vegetables are softened, about 5 minutes. Remove and cool.

2. Meanwhile, season the beef with salt and pepper or rub. When the vegetables are cool, arrange the beef and vegetable pieces on metal or sturdy wooden skewers, alternating the ingredients and dividing them evenly among the skewers.

3. Set up the smoker using the wood chips and smoke the skewers until the beef is done to your liking and the vegetables are tender, about 15 minutes for medium-rare beef; 20 minutes for medium beef, and longer for more well-done beef. Serve hot from the smoker.

Flank Steak and Roasted Red Onion Sandwiches

2 teaspoons olive oil

1 medium red onion (about 8 ounces), sliced ¼ inch thick

Kosher salt

Freshly ground black pepper

2 tablespoons mayonnaise

1½ tablespoons grainy or Dijon mustard

Finely chopped bottled pepperoncini or cherry peppers to taste, optional

2 kaiser, hero, or sourdough rolls, split, or 4 slices coarse-textured bread

8 to 10 slices smoked flank steak, warm or cold

Sliced tomato

When you find yourself with leftover smoked flank steak (page 188), or any grilled or broiled flank steak, look no further for the best-tasting way to use them up. Roasted red onions are a wonderful accompaniment for any grilled or smoked steak. They also make an unusual and delicious condiment for just about any meat-filled sandwich.

MAKES 2 SANDWICHES

1. Preheat the oven to 400°F. Brush a baking sheet lightly with half of the olive oil. Arrange the onion slices on the baking sheet and brush the tops with the remaining olive oil. Season lightly (the onions will shrivel up quite a bit and that will intensify the seasoning) with salt and pepper. Roast 10 minutes. Flip the onions and continue roasting until they are well browned and tender, 8 to 10 minutes.

2. While the onions are roasting, stir the mayonnaise, mustard, and pepperoncini, if using, together in a small bowl.

3. Toast the bread of your choice; in the toaster for sliced bread or under the broiler for rolls. Slather one side of each roll with half the sauce. Pile the beef slices over the sauce and top with tomato slices, roasted onions, and the other piece of bread.

Butterflied Leg of Lamb with Roasted Potatoes, Greek Style

Lemon, garlic, and oregano are the hallmarks of Greek cuisine. Here those three work beautifully with a tender leg of lamb. The potatoes that roast while the lamb is smoking are also seasoned in typical Greek fashion, with lemon juice and olive oil at the end of their time in the oven. Read through the recipe carefully before you start to cook. It explains how to get a crusty, juicy leg of lamb and golden brown potatoes to the table at the same time.

MAKES 6 SERVINGS

Butterflied smoked leg of lamb, about 2½ pounds

2 teaspoons kosher salt, plus more for seasoning the sauce

½ teaspoon freshly ground black pepper, plus more for seasoning the sauce

FOR THE POTATOES

4 medium russet potatoes (about 2½ pounds)

1 cup homemade or canned reduced-sodium chicken broth

¼ cup olive oil

2 teaspoons kosher salt

½ teaspoon freshly ground black pepper

2 tablespoons oak, hickory, or maple wood chips

⅓ cup plus one tablespoon extra virgin olive oil

5 tablespoons fresh lemon juice

1 tablespoon dried oregano

4 garlic cloves, minced

1. Pat the leg of lamb dry with paper towels. Rub 2 teaspoons salt and ½ teaspoon pepper into all sides of the lamb. Let the lamb stand at room temperature for 45 minutes or, preferably, refrigerate for up to one day. Bring refrigerated lamb to room temperature before smoking.

2. Heat the oven to 400°F. Peel the potatoes and cut them in half crosswise. Cut each half lengthwise into four wedges. Toss the potatoes together with the chicken broth and 2 tablespoons of the olive oil in a 13 × 9-inch baking dish. Season with 2 teaspoons salt and ½ teaspoon pepper and toss again. Roast until the potatoes are tender and lightly browned, stirring gently once or twice, about 45 minutes.

3. As soon as the potatoes are in the oven, start the lamb. Set up the smoker using the wood chips and smoke the lamb

according to the directions on page 4 until an instant-read thermometer inserted into the thickest part of the lamb registers 130°F (medium-rare), 40 to 45 minutes.

4. Meanwhile, make the sauce for the lamb. Stir ⅓ cup extra virgin olive oil, 3 tablespoons lemon juice, the oregano, and garlic together in a small bowl. Season to taste with salt and pepper.

5. When the potatoes are tender, toss them very gently with the 2 tablespoons olive oil and 2 tablespoons lemon juice. Return them to the oven and roast until golden brown, about 10 minutes.

> Choose a butterflied leg of lamb of more or less even thickness if you want an evenly cooked piece of lamb. If, however, your lamb eaters like everything from medium-rare to well-done, a cut of uneven thickness will give you everything you need.

6. Just after returning the potatoes to the oven, heat a large, heavy skillet over medium-high heat. Pour in the remaining tablespoon extra virgin olive oil. When the lamb is ready, remove it from the smoker with tongs and lay it in the skillet. Cook just until browned on both sides, about 2 minutes per side. Let rest 10 minutes before serving.

7. Carve the lamb into ½-inch slices and arrange them overlapping on a platter. Spoon a little of the olive oil sauce over the lamb and pass the rest separately. Spoon the potatoes gently onto a separate platter, or the same platter as the lamb if there is room. Serve the potatoes hot.

vegetables and side dishes

Plum Tomatoes

Plum tomatoes, with their meaty texture and compact shape, make excellent candidates for smoking. Even if you need to smoke only half a batch of tomatoes to serve as a side dish or in order to make salsa, go ahead and smoke a whole batch. Turn the unused tomatoes into Smoked Tomato Sauce (page 14) and pop it in the freezer.

How Many? Up to eight good-sized plum tomatoes (about 2 pounds) will fit on the smoker rack at one time.

How Long? Until the tomatoes are softened, but not mushy; 10 minutes over the heat after closing the smoker lid and about 20 minutes off the heat with the smoker lid closed.

Which Wood? Because of the relatively short smoking time, use an assertive wood like 2 tablespoons of hickory or mesquite wood chips.

Cut the cores from the tomatoes with a paring knife, then cut the tomatoes in half through the core end. Squeeze out the seeds and juice. Line the tomato halves up side by side and cut side up on the smoking rack.

Season the cut side of the tomatoes with a generous sprinkling of salt and pepper.

Check the tomatoes for doneness after they've been standing off the heat for 10 minutes.

Serve smoked tomatoes as a side dish with just about any grilled or roasted meat, poultry, or seafood dish, or use them in **Smoky-Spicy Salsa** (page 21) or **Smoked Tomato Sauce** (page 14).

Bell Peppers

How Many? Up to 3 large bell peppers, cut into segments, as described below, will fit on the smoker rack at one time.

How Long? About 20 minutes for crisp-tender peppers or up to 30 minutes for tender peppers with wrinkled skins.

Which Wood? The inside surface of the pepper will absorb a lot of smoke flavor. To prevent overwhelming the pepper with smoke, choose a small amount, about 1 table-spoon, of mild wood chips like alder or cherry.

Trim the peppers into segments as follows: with the pepper stem side down on the cutting board, cut along the indentations in the pepper until you reach the core. Gently pull off each section of the pepper. You will be left with just a core, seeds, and stem, which you discard.

It is best to **season** the peppers after cooking, as raw peppers won't absorb much seasoning. When the peppers are done smoking, give them a light rub of olive oil and a sprinkling of salt and pepper.

Start the peppers skin side down on the rack.

Check the peppers for doneness after 20 minutes.

Serve the peppers as a side dish or as part of an appetizer platter that could also feature Monterey Jack cheese, spiced olives, and **In-Flight Almonds** (page 57).

Whether I'm roasting red, yellow, or green peppers (see page 54), or smoking them, I like to cut them into natural-looking shapes rather than in half through the core. Cutting them this way also reduces waste.

Corn on the Cob

While putting the recipes together for this book, I would often say to myself, "If there's one reason to buy a stovetop smoker, this is it." If I had to actually narrow it down to just one reason it would be tough, but smoking corn on the cob is definitely in the top five. The kernels keep their sweetness, which is intensified by smoking, and their crunch and juiciness. Stripped from the cob—a very simple procedure—the kernels are an amazing addition to all kinds of salads, soups, and salsas. When it comes to most bang for the buck, smoked corn is leader of the pack.

How Many? Up to four ears of corn will fit on the smoker rack at one time.

How Long? Until the kernels are tender and browned, about 20 minutes.

Which Wood? Choose 1½ to 2½ tablespoons of milder wood chips, like alder or cherry. Or go with the obvious—corncob chips.

Trim the husk and as much of the silk as you can from the ears.

Season the corn by rubbing the ears lightly with olive or vegetable oil; other seasonings will not penetrate the corn kernels while they're still on the cob.

Check the corn for doneness after about 15 minutes.

Serve corn on the cob hot out of the smoker, brushed lightly with butter and sprinkled with salt. Once you scrape the kernels from the cob, there are a thousand things to do with them, like sauté them with diced red bell pepper for a quick side dish; stir them into your favorite store-bought or homemade salsa; sprinkle them into seafood chowder; or include them in just about any quesadilla filling, including the **Smoked Chicken and Black Bean Quesadillas** (page 46). Or you can use smoked corn kernels in:

Mexican Tortilla and Smoked Corn Soup (page 66)

Smoked Corn and Black Bean Salad (page 80)

Gold Nugget Potato Pancakes (page 225)

NOTE: Four ears of corn will yield about 1⅓ cups smoked kernels.

Eggplant

How Many? One 1-pound eggplant, cut into ¾-inch slices (about 12 slices) will fit on the smoker rack.

How Long? Until the eggplant is tender and lightly browned, about 20 minutes over the heat. To let the eggplant absorb more smoke flavor, remove the smoker from the heat and let it stand 5 to 10 minutes with the smoker top closed.

Which Wood? Eggplant is amenable to all kinds of wood. If you plan to serve it on its own as a side dish, choose milder wood chips like 1½ tablespoons of alder or apple. If it is headed into a well-seasoned dish, like the **Eggplant Dip** on page 55, use a wood with kick, like pecan or mesquite.

Trim the stem and opposite end; leave the peel on or remove it, as you prefer. The skin will not become tender after smoking, so remove it with a vegetable peeler if this bothers you.

Season the eggplant slices and rid them of their bitterness by sprinkling a baking sheet with a generous amount of kosher salt. Lay the eggplant over the salt and salt the tops generously. Let them stand 1 to 2 hours, then slide them into a colander. Rinse them well under plenty of cold running water. Drain in the colander, then pat them dry with paper towels.

Check the eggplant for doneness after 15 minutes. If the eggplant slices near the center are browning quicker than those around the edges, rotate their positions with tongs.

To salt or not to salt? Some cooks swear by salting their eggplant before cooking, claiming the salt draws out bitter juices and renders a kinder, gentler eggplant. Others dismiss that as hogwash. I usually salt, rinse, and drain eggplant, but will always do so to eggplant destined for the smoker after the experience I

The instructions here are for smoking Italian eggplant—the larger, purple-skinned variety that is the most common. If you grow or have access to more exotic forms of the vegetable, like baby eggplants; long, thin Japanese eggplants; or rounder, plumper white eggplants, you can smoke those too. Cut any long, thin eggplant in half lengthwise rather than into slices before salting and smoking.

had testing the recipes for this book. The first time I smoked eggplant it was, to put it mildly, a disappointment—mushy and exceedingly bitter. I tried salting it as described here and the results were excellent— smoky-sweet and with a firmer, more pleasant texture. Thinking this might be a fluke, I chose two neighboring eggplants from the bin on my next trip to the supermarket, salted one and let the other ride au naturel. No blindfold was needed for the taste test—the salted eggplant ruled.

Serve the eggplant as a side dish, in salads, or as part of an antipasto platter. Or dice it and add it to tomato sauce for pasta. Heaven is a smoked eggplant, fresh mozzarella, and sliced ripe tomato sandwich on a crunchy roll, especially when you season the tomato slices with very good olive oil, coarse sea salt, and tons of fresh basil. Seventh heaven is when the tomato is picked right from the vine and you're enjoying the sandwich in the shade with a freezing cold beer instead of cutting the lawn.

Red, Yellow, Spanish, or Sweet Onions

How Many? Up to two medium (6 ounces each) onions, sliced a scant ½ inch thick (about 12 slices), will fit on the smoker rack at one time.

How Long? Until lightly browned and tender, about 20 minutes.

Which Wood? Complement the natural sweetness of onions with about 2 tablespoons of apple or corncob chips.

Trim the root end from the onions and peel away the papery skin and outermost ring. Slice them as evenly as you can, just under a half-inch thick, transferring the slices to the smoker rack as you work to keep them intact.

Season the onions by brushing them lightly with olive oil and sprinkling them liberally with salt and pepper.

Check the onions for doneness after 15 minutes.

Serve smoked onion slices with grilled meat or poultry, toss them in a salad, or use them in sandwiches. Always make more than you think you need—you'll find a million uses for them.

Choose your favorite from the above. I didn't notice much of a difference between yellow and Spanish onions, but red onions gave a slightly sweeter and sharper end result. Sweet onions, like Vidalias, make wonderful eating on their own or in sandwiches or dips.

Portobello Mushroom Caps

How Many? Up to four 5-inch caps will fit on the smoker rack at one time.

How Long? Until tender but firm and evenly browned, about 20 minutes.

Which Wood? Mushrooms caps are very porous and will absorb a lot of flavor. To avoid oversmoking, use 1 tablespoon of alder or cherry wood chips.

Trim and discard the stems from the portobellos. Peel the caps by turning them gill side up and gently pulling at some of the overhanging peel; it will remove easily in wide strips, leaving a pure white cap. Scrape out all the dark brown gills from the underside of the cap with a teaspoon.

Rub both sides of each trimmed 5-inch mushroom cap with 1 tablespoon olive oil (which it will quickly absorb) and sprinkle it generously with kosher salt and freshly ground black pepper.

Check the mushroom caps for tenderness after 15 minutes.

Serve sliced smoked portobello mushrooms as a side dish for grilled pork or beef, or in salads. Whole, they make excellent burgers. Or use them to make portobello BLTs with sliced tomatoes, leaves of Boston lettuce, crispy bacon, and lots of mayo. Or use them in **Scrambled Eggs with Smoked Portobellos, Spinach, and Fontina Cheese** (page 226).

Whole Garlic Bulbs

How Many? Up to 12 medium heads of garlic (a little over 1 pound) will fit on the smoker rack at one time.

How Long? Until the innermost cloves of garlic are soft when you poke them with a paring knife; about 45 minutes over heat and 15 minutes off the heat with the smoker lid closed. See Combo-Cooking if your garlic is not tender at that point.

Which Wood? Just about anything goes with garlic—from the subtle smoke of 1½ tablespoons of alder or cherry wood chips to the kick of 2 tablespoons mesquite and hickory wood chips.

Trim the pointy tops—about a half-inch or so—of the heads to expose the individual cloves. Gently rub off as much of the papery outer layers as possible without breaking off the cloves. This will allow the smoky flavor to penetrate the cloves more fully.

Start trimmed heads of garlic on the smoker rack cut side up and **season** them by drizzling a little olive oil in between the cloves and sprinkling them with salt and pepper.

Combo-Cooking: If the innermost cloves of garlic aren't tender after 45 minutes of smoking and 15 minutes of resting, preheat the oven to 300°F. Transfer the garlic heads to a small baking dish or glass pie plate and pour in enough water to

If you've ever enjoyed roasted garlic, you know that slow-cooking tames the beast in raw garlic. Long, slow smoking also softens the cloves to a buttery consistency—

TO SMOKE GARLIC CLOVES

This is a very handy thing to know if you don't plan to serve whole heads of garlic, especially if your supermarket sells jars of peeled garlic. Before you set up the smoker, bring a small saucepan of salted water to a boil. Add up to 8 ounces (about 1½ cups) peeled garlic cloves and cook 1½ minutes. Drain, rinse briefly under cold water, and pat dry with paper towels. Put the garlic cloves in a perforated aluminum pan and rub them lightly with olive oil. Season with salt and pepper and smoke until tender, 35 to 40 minutes, using the wood chips of your choice.

handy for whipping into mashed potatoes (page 230) or spreading on bruschetta (page 82)—and adds the unmistakable flavor that only smoking can. Choose heads of garlic with small cloves—they will be easier to smoke until tender. I've smoked whole heads of garlic several times; sometimes they're fine right out of the smoker and sometimes they need a little stint in the oven. (See Combo-Cooking if your garlic cloves aren't tender after 45 minutes in the smoker.) The box describes how to smoke individual peeled cloves of garlic.

fill the dish ½ inch. Cover the dish tightly with aluminum foil and bake until tender. After smoking, this shouldn't be longer than 20 minutes.

Serve whole heads of smoked garlic to garlic-loving friends as a side dish at anything from a backyard barbecue to a sit-down dinner. Guests can pluck off the cloves one at a time and squeeze the marvelous, butter-smooth clove from its papery wrapper. Give each person a tiny plate with some fruity olive oil and let them dunk their bread, then spread it with the garlic. You can extract the pulp from any leftover cloves and put it to any number of delicious uses, like seasoning soups, salad dressings, or sautéed vegetables. Or squeeze the pulp from about half a head's worth of garlic and beat it into a stick of softened butter. Season the butter with salt, pepper, and, if you like, a squirt of lemon juice. (Delicious on a grilled steak.) In short, you can used smoked garlic cloves just about anywhere you use regular garlic. For a couple of ideas to get you started, check out **World's Best Garlic Bread** (page 52) and **Smoky Caesar Salad** (page 83).

Tofu

How Many? Up to two 1-pound pieces of tofu, if you're smoking them whole, or one pound if you're slicing them before smoking (see box).

How Long? 12 minutes over medium heat, then 5 minutes off the heat with the smoker lid closed.

Which Wood? Opt for mild choices, like 1½ tablespoons alder or cherry wood chips or 1 tablespoon oak wood chips.

Serve smoked tofu as you would regular tofu, or use it in **Crispy-Velvet Tofu with Warm Spinach Salad** on page 233.

Smoking the whole brick of tofu, then slicing it, gives the tofu a mild smoky flavor. For a more pronounced flavor, cut the tofu into four even slices and lay them on their sides on the smoking rack.

Corn, Cheddar, and Red Onion Tortilla

You may think of a tortilla as a round, thin bread made from cornmeal or wheat flour, but in Spain a tortilla is a thick, baked omelet, similar to the Italian frittata. They are usually loaded with potatoes, sautéed onions, and just about anything else you can think of. This combination of Cheddar cheese and smoked corn is not traditional by any means, but it is absolutely irresistible. Tortillas are the perfect food for brunch, dinner, or a buffet. They're easy to put together, almost foolproof, and if you serve them at room temperature—my favorite way—they can be made hours in advance.

MAKES 6 SERVINGS

3 ears smoked corn on the cob

4 medium red-skinned new potatoes or Yukon gold potatoes (about 12 ounces)

5 tablespoons extra virgin olive oil

1 yellow onion, cut in half, then sliced about ½ inch

1½ teaspoons kosher salt, plus more for seasoning the vegetables

Freshly ground black pepper

10 large eggs

½ cup milk

3 cups coarsely grated medium-sharp Cheddar cheese

1. Smoke the corn according to the directions on page 214. When cool enough to handle, strip the kernels from the cobs.

2. Pour enough cold water over the potatoes in a 3-quart saucepan to cover them by a few inches. Bring the water to a boil over medium-high heat, then adjust the heat so the water is at a gentle boil. Cook until the potatoes are tender when poked with a fork, 20 to 30 minutes, depending on the size of the potatoes. Drain the potatoes and cool them to room temperature. Peel them, if you like, and cut them into ½-inch slices.

3. Position the rack in the center of the oven and preheat the oven to 325°F. Heat 3 tablespoons of the olive oil in a large, ovenproof skillet—cast iron is ideal—over medium heat. Stir in the onion, season lightly with salt and pepper and cook, stirring occasionally, until they are wilted but not browned, about 6 minutes. Beat the eggs, milk, and 1½ teaspoons salt together in a large bowl until thoroughly blended. Stir in the corn kernels and cheese.

4. Add the remaining 2 tablespoons olive oil to the pan, and swirl it around to coat the sides as much as possible. Gently stir the sliced potatoes into the skillet and cook them a minute or two to warm them through.

5. Reduce the heat to medium-low and pour the egg mixture into the skillet. Don't stir. In about a minute, the egg should begin to bubble in a few spots around and near the edges. If it starts to bubble sooner, lift the pan from the heat and reduce the heat slightly. Wait a minute and return the pan to the heat. Cook until the edges are lightly browned (check by carefully slipping a thin metal spatula or knife along the edge of the tortilla), about 5 minutes.

6. Set the skillet in the oven and cook until the top is puffed and brown and the center is firm to the touch, 25 to 30 minutes.

7. Serve the tortilla hot after letting it rest 5 minutes, warm after resting 30 to 40 minutes, or cooled completely to room temperature. In any case, run a thin, flexible spatula around the sides, then underneath, to make sure the tortilla hasn't stuck to the pan. Serve the hot tortilla right from the pan. You can serve the warm or room temperature tortilla from the pan as well or, if you're feeling adventurous and have strong wrists, invert it onto a plate as follows: make sure the tortilla is not stuck to any part of the pan. Cover the pan with a plate that is at least 2 inches wider than the pan. Working about a foot over a counter, hold the handle of the skillet with one hand and clamp the plate over the top of the skillet with the other. Invert the skillet over the plate in one quick motion, then lower the plate onto the counter and lift off the skillet. You can also cut the tortilla into wedges in the pan and lift them to individual serving plates.

NOTE: To prevent this or any other tortilla/frittata from sticking, start with a well-seasoned cast-iron skillet or heavy, completely ovenproof skillet. (No plastic handles!) Then, don't peek for a few minutes after pouring in the egg. Let the egg form a lightly browned underside before shaking the pan or checking for brownness.

Gold Nugget Potato Pancakes

2 ears smoked corn on the
    cob

1 large (12-ounce) russet
    potato

½ teaspoon kosher salt

¼ teaspoon freshly ground
    black pepper

1 tablespoon unsalted butter

1 tablespoon vegetable oil

1. Smoke the corn according to the directions on page 214. When cool enough to handle, strip the kernels from the cobs.

2. Just before you're ready to make the pancakes, peel the potato and grate it coarsely into a small bowl. Add the corn, salt, and pepper, and stir until the kernels are distributed throughout the potato. The potato will start to turn brown almost instantly, but this will not affect the flavor. However, if the shredded potatoes sit too long, the finished pancakes will take on a grayish tint.

3. Heat the butter and oil in a large, heavy griddle or skillet—cast iron is ideal—over medium-low heat until the butter is foaming. To make large pancakes, fill a ¼-cup measure with the potato mixture and scrape it into the skillet in a mound. Press the mixture gently to make a pancake about 3 inches in diameter and ½ inch thick. Cook as many pancakes in one batch as will fit without touching. Cook until the underside is deep golden brown and crispy, about 6 minutes. Flip and cook the other side until deep golden brown and the potatoes in the center are tender, about 5 minutes. Keep cooked pancakes warm on a baking sheet in an oven turned to the lowest setting while cooking the remaining pancakes.

NOTE: Use a 1-tablespoon measure to make miniature (about ¾-inch) pancakes. Press them just enough to flatten them into an even layer. Cook until golden brown and crispy on both sides, 4 to 5 minutes per side.

Putting together these crispy, tender potato pancakes studded with kernels of smoked corn is a pretty low-tech affair: you'll need a bowl, a grater, and a heavy pan. Make little potato pancakes for hors d'oeuvres and top them with a small piece of smoked salmon and a mini-dollop of sour cream, or make larger pancakes as a side dish for saucy things like pot roast or braised short ribs.

MAKES EIGHT
3-INCH PANCAKES OR
TWENTY-FOUR 1-INCH
PANCAKES

Scrambled Eggs with Smoked Portobellos, Spinach, and Fontina Cheese

It's a culinary cliché to say that portobellos are meaty, but in this simple egg dish you would swear they resemble smoked ham—a classic pairing with scrambled eggs. Experiment with other cheeses like Brie or Camembert and by adding tender vegetables like peas or diced tomatoes during the last minute of cooking.

MAKES 2 SERVINGS

2 smoked portobello mushroom caps

6 large eggs

1 teaspooon kosher salt

¼ teaspoon freshly ground black pepper

1 cup grated fontina or Gouda cheese

½ cup chopped cooked spinach, fresh or frozen

2 tablespoons unsalted butter

1. Smoke the portobellos according to the directions on page 218. Cool them to room temperature and cut them into ½-inch dice.

2. Beat the eggs, 1 tablespoon water, salt, and pepper together in a mixing bowl until no streaks of white or yolk remain. Fold in the mushrooms, cheese, and spinach.

3. Heat the butter in a heavy, large nonstick pan over medium-low heat until foaming gently. Pour in the egg mixture and cook, stirring constantly, just until the eggs are set but still moist, about 8 minutes. Serve immediately.

Spaghetti with Portobellos and Parsley Pesto

6 smoked portobello
   mushroom caps (each
   about 3 inches across)

¾ teaspoon kosher salt, plus
   more for cooking the
   pasta

Leaves from 1 bunch flat-leaf
   parsley (about 2 cups),
   washed and patted dry

½ cup walnut pieces

3 garlic cloves

¼ cup plus 2 tablespoons
   extra virgin olive oil

¼ cup grated Parmesan
   cheese, plus more for
   passing at the table

1 pound spaghetti

Parsley, mushrooms, and garlic have a magical relationship, as a panful of button mushrooms sautéed with olive oil and garlic and sprinkled with a little chopped parsley will show. This more sophisticated take on the theme matches smoked portobello mushroom caps with a mildly garlicky pesto that uses fresh flat-leaf parsley in place of the traditional basil.

MAKES 6 SERVINGS

1. Smoke the mushroom caps according to the directions on page 218. Cool them to room temperature. Cut the caps in half crosswise, or into thirds if they're more than 3 inches in diameter, then into ¼-inch strips.

2. Bring a large pot of salted water to a boil. Meanwhile, make the pesto, by chopping the parsley, walnuts, and garlic coarsely in a food processor fitted with the metal blade. With the motor running, pour the oil into the bowl and continue processing until the parsley is finely chopped. Stop once or twice to scrape down the sides of the bowl. Add ¼ cup Parmesan and process just until incorporated. Scrape the pesto into a small bowl, season to taste with salt and set aside. The pesto may be made up to two days in advance. Refrigerate it with a piece of plastic wrap pressed directly to the surface to prevent discoloration.

3. Stir the spaghetti into the boiling water. Continue stirring gently until the water returns to a boil. Cook, stirring once in a while, until the spaghetti is al dente, about 8 minutes. Ladle off and reserve about 1 cup of the pasta cooking water. Drain the pasta thoroughly in a colander and return it to the pot over low heat.

4. Stir just enough of the reserved pasta cooking water into the spaghetti to moisten it. Toss in the mushrooms and stir until warmed through. Stir in the parsley pesto and enough of the reserved pasta cooking liquid to make a sauce that evenly and lightly coats the pasta. Season with salt, if necessary. Serve the spaghetti on a large warm platter and pass additional grated Parmesan.

Ultimate Corn Bread

3 ears smoked corn on the cob

Vegetable cooking spray or
    melted butter

1¼ cups yellow cornmeal

1 cup all-purpose flour

¼ cup sugar

2 teaspoons baking powder

1 teaspoon kosher salt

½ teaspoon baking soda

¾ cup milk

½ cup sour cream

2 large eggs

This bread is thick, moist, and loaded with a double shot of corn flavor that comes from sweet and smoky corn kernels and golden cornmeal. Day-old Ultimate Corn Bread is delicious sliced thick and toasted, then schmeared with butter and, if you go for such things, grape jelly.

MAKES ONE
8-INCH SQUARE LOAF,
SIXTEEN 2 × 2-INCH
PIECES

1. Smoke the corn according to the directions on page 214. Cool to room temperature and scrape the kernels off the cobs.

2. Set the rack in the center position and preheat the oven to 400°F. Grease an 8-inch square cake pan with vegetable cooking spray or melted butter.

3. Stir the cornmeal, flour, sugar, baking powder, salt, and baking soda together in a mixing bowl. Toss the corn in the dry ingredients until coated. If necessary, break the kernels apart with your fingers. Beat the milk, sour cream, and eggs together in a separate bowl until no streaks of yolk or white are visible. Pour the egg mixture into the dry ingredients and stir together with a rubber spatula, scraping the sides and bottom of the bowl, just until blended. It's fine if the batter is lumpy. Scrape the batter into the prepared pan and bake until the top is light golden brown and the center springs back when pressed with a finger, about 25 minutes.

4. Cool the corn bread on a rack at least 30 minutes before serving. Serve warm or at room temperature.

Garlic Mashed Potatoes

You may have enjoyed "garlic mashed" made with garlic that's been roasted or sautéed, which mellows its bite and adds sweetness. Smoking garlic does the same, and adds the tantalizing flavor of smoke to boot. Make more of these than you think you'll need. Smoked garlic mashed are delicious served with meat loaf, especially if you pair both with the Brown Gravy on page 20 or the Smoked Tomato Sauce on page 14.

MAKES 4 SERVINGS

20 cloves smoked garlic

2 pounds large Yukon gold potatoes, peeled and cut in half

Kosher salt

½ cup milk

3 tablespoons unsalted butter or olive oil

Freshly ground black pepper

1. Smoke the garlic according to the directions on page 219 and cool to room temperature.

2. Pour enough cold water over the potatoes in a large saucepan to cover by at least 2 inches. Add a good amount of salt and bring to a boil. Adjust the heat to a gentle boil, partially cover the pan and cook just until the potatoes are tender when poked with a fork, 20 to 25 minutes, depending on the size of your potatoes.

3. While the potatoes are cooking, combine the garlic and milk in a blender jar and blend at low speed until the garlic is finely chopped. Set aside.

4. Drain the potatoes thoroughly. Pour the milk and garlic mixture into the saucepan, drop in the butter and swirl until the butter is melted. Return the potatoes to the pan. Mash the potatoes with a potato masher for a coarse texture, or beat them with a handheld mixer for smoother, fluffier texture. Add salt and pepper to taste and serve hot.

Vegetarian Chiles Rellenos

FOR THE TOMATO SAUCE

3 tablespoons vegetable oil

1 small red onion, diced ¼ inch

2 garlic cloves, chopped

Kosher salt

One 26-ounce can or two 15-ounce cans chopped tomatoes and their liquid

¼ teaspoon red pepper flakes

2 tablespoons chopped fresh cilantro

FOR THE CHILES

8 medium (about 7 inches long) poblano or Anaheim chiles (about 1 pound)

1½ tablespoons mesquite or hickory wood chips

One 15-ounce can black beans, drained and rinsed

2 cups grated Monterey Jack cheese

1 red bell pepper, roasted and peeled (see page 54), cut into ½-inch dice or ⅔ cup diced (½-inch) bottled roasted red peppers

3 medium scallions, trimmed and chopped

3 tablespoons chopped fresh cilantro

Anaheim peppers are mildly and sweetly spicy. When smoked, they take on another flavor dimension. I love this version of stuffed chiles, filled with beans, roasted peppers, and cheese, but if you have a favorite meaty filling recipe that you usually use for stuffed peppers, fill the peppers with that instead. You'll be surprised how much better the same filling will taste in smoked chiles.

MAKES 4 MAIN COURSE SERVINGS

1. Make the sauce: Heat the oil in a medium saucepan over medium heat. Stir in the onion and garlic and season them lightly with salt. Cook, stirring, until the onion is lightly browned, about 8 minutes. Pour in the tomatoes and ½ cup water. Add the red pepper flakes and season lightly with salt. Bring to a boil. Adjust the heat so the sauce is simmering and cook, stirring occasionally, until the sauce is lightly thickened, about 15 minutes. Remove from the heat and stir in 2 tablespoons chopped cilantro.

2. Lay the chiles on a flat surface to see on which side they rest most naturally. This will make them easier to stuff and serve. Using that side as the bottom, make a slit along the top from the stem end to opposite end. Set up the smoker using the wood chips and smoke the peppers according to the directions on page 213 until softened, about 20 minutes. Remove the peppers and cool them to room temperature.

3. Stir the beans, 1½ cups of the cheese, the roasted pepper, scallions, 3 tablespoons cilantro, and ½ cup of the tomato sauce together in a mixing bowl. Gently open the peppers and scrape out the seeds and membranes from around the core. Divide the stuffing among the chiles. Gently press the chiles back into their natural shape, leaving a strip of the filling exposed along the length of the slit.

4. Spread the remaining sauce over the bottom of a 9 × 13-inch baking dish. Nestle the stuffed chiles into the sauce. Top the chiles with the remaining cheese, pressing it lightly onto the exposed filling. Cover the dish with aluminum foil and bake until the sauce is bubbling, about 35 minutes. Uncover and bake 10 minutes. Let stand 10 minutes before serving.

Crispy-Velvet Tofu with Warm Spinach Salad

I pound extra-firm smoked tofu

I½ pounds fresh spinach, preferably the flat-leaf variety, or I pound baby spinach leaves

¼ cup cornstarch

I½ teaspoons kosher salt

¼ cup vegetable oil

I tablespoon Asian sesame oil

2 scallions, trimmed and sliced very thinly

I-inch piece fresh ginger, peeled and cut into very thin strips

2 garlic cloves, peeled and minced

2 tablespoons soy sauce

2 teaspoons rice vinegar or white wine vinegar

I tablespoon toasted sesame seeds, optional

MAKES 2 MAIN COURSE OR 6 FIRST COURSE SERVINGS

1. Smoke the tofu according to the directions on page 221, leaving it whole for a milder smoke flavor, cutting it into 6 even slices first for a more pronounced flavor. Cool completely.

2. Cut the tofu into 6 even slices if you haven't already done so. Lay the tofu slices on a double thickness of paper towels to drain as much moisture from them as possible. Turn the slices once or twice.

3. While the tofu is drying, clean the spinach: remove any stems from the flat-leaf spinach. (This isn't necessary if you're using baby spinach.) Fill a large bowl or, preferably, a sink with cool water. Add the spinach, swish it around gently but thoroughly, then let it stand a few minutes to allow any dirt or sand to settle to the bottom. Scoop out the leaves into a colander to drain. Dry the leaves in batches in a salad spinner and set aside. The spinach can be washed and dried up to one day in advance. Store in the refrigerator until needed.

4. Stir the cornstarch and salt together on a wide plate and coat all sides of the tofu slices with the mixture. Tap off any excesss. Heat the vegetable oil in a large, deep skillet over medium heat until a corner of one of the tofu slices gives off a lively sizzle when dipped into the oil. Carefully slip the slices into the oil and cook, turning once, until light golden brown on both sides, about 10 minutes. Adjust the heat as they cook so the tofu sizzles gently as it cooks. If the tofu doesn't sizzle at all, raise the heat; if it is splattering or bubbling wildly, reduce the heat.

5. Lift the tofu slices from the oil with a slotted spatula and let them drain for a second or two over the skillet. Drain them on a baking sheet lined with a double thickness of paper towels. Pour off all but one tablespoon of the oil, and add the sesame oil. Stir in the scallions, ginger, and garlic, and cook, stirring, until the garlic turns very light brown, about 1 minute.

6. Remove the pan from the heat, add the spinach leaves, and toss with two wooden spoons until the spinach is wilted and the scallions, ginger, and garlic are distributed throughout the leaves. Drizzle the soy sauce and vinegar over the spinach and toss again. Mound the spinach over the center of warm plates and set the tofu over it. Serve warm, sprinkled with the sesame seeds, if using.

Index

basil (*continued*)

    in bronzed sea scallops with chunky tomato vinaigrette, 148–49

    in orzo salad with smoked mozzarella, broccoli, and garlic chips, 87–88

    in pesto, 63

    in rigatoni with smoked turkey and hot cherry peppers, 126–27

beans, *see specific beans*

beef, 185–95

    barbecued short ribs of, 202–3

    brisket, smoking of, 186–87

    jerky, 42–43

    pepper, and red onion kabobs, 206

beef tenderloin steaks:

    smoking of, 190–91

    triple mushroom, 204–5

best-of-the-Carolinas barbecue sauce, 19

    in pulled pork, 170–71

black bean(s):

    and smoked chicken quesadillas, 46–47

    and smoked corn salad, 80–81

    in vegetarian chiles rellenos, 231–32

bluefish, smoked:

    fillet, 136

    in MV fish cakes, 159–60

Boston lettuce:

    in smoked chicken, pecan, and Gruyère salad, 74–75

    in smoked corn and black bean salad, 80–81

    in smoked trout fillets with baby greens and horseradish whipped cream, 33–34

bow tie pasta salad with smoked shrimp and cherry tomatoes, 85–86

brandy, in prune-stuffed loin pork chops, 174–75

bread:

    ultimate corn, 229

    world's best garlic, 52

brining, 11, 12

broccoli:

    orzo salad with smoked mozzarella, garlic chips and, 87–88

    in tea-smoked shrimp and asparagus stir-fry, 150–51

bronzed sea scallops with chunky tomato vinaigrette, 148–49

brown gravy, 20

bruschetta, 82

butter:

    Casino, smoked clams on the half shell with, 38

    herb, for whole poultry, 101

butterflied leg of lamb with roasted potatoes, Greek style, 208–9

cabbage:

    apple-cured pork tenderloin with sweet and sour, 176–77

    Napa, in tea-smoked duck with Asian slaw, 128–29

    savoy, *see* savoy cabbage

    smoked cod with bacon and, 152–53

Caesar salad, smoky, 83–84

cannellini beans:

    in monster minestrone, 60–62

    in smoked salmon gone to heaven, 144–45

    in tuna and white bean salad, 82

Carolina style "mop" sauce, 167

    in pulled pork, 170–71

Casino butter, smoked clams on the half shell with, 38

casserole:

    country style pork and white bean, 178–80

    smoked chicken, string bean, and cauliflower, 121–22

cauliflower, smoked chicken and string bean casserole, 121–22

cayenne chiles, in Southwestern rub, 28

celery seed slaw, 90

chard, Swiss, in smoked cod with bacon and cabbage, 152–53

in crispy-velvet tofu with warm spinach salad, 233–34

in shredded chicken with peanut sauce, 48–49

in tea-smoked shrimp and asparagus stir-fry, 150–51

glaze:

maple mustard, 168

quickie teriyaki, 167–68

see also sauces

gold nugget potato pancakes, 225

Gouda cheese, in scrambled eggs with smoked portobellos, spinach, and fontina cheese, 226

Granny Smith apples:

in chef Walsh's swordfish with radicchio and papaya salad, 155–56

in smoked chicken, pecan, and Gruyère salad, 74–75

gravy, brown, 20

great Northern beans, in country style pork and white bean casserole, 178–80

Greek style butterflied leg of lamb with roasted potatoes, 208–9

green goddess sauce, 17

greens, baby, smoked trout fillets with horseradish whipped cream and, 33–34

Gruyère, smoked chicken, and pecan salad, 74–75

habanero chiles, in herby chicken breasts with pipérade, 114–15

haddock, smoked:

fillet, 135

in smoked cod with bacon and cabbage, 152–53

half-and-half:

in smoked pork medallions with shameless succotash, 181

in smoky mussel chowder, 72–73

ham, smoked:

in herby chicken breasts with pipérade, 114–15

in quail with wild rice stuffing, 130–31

hamburgers:

seasonings for, 195

smoking of, 195

hash, smoked turkey, 125

hazelnut, toasted, shredded duck, and watercress salad, 76–77

herb(y):

butter, for whole poultry, 101

chicken breasts with pipérade, 114–15

-mushroom rub, *see* mushroom-herb rub

see also specific herbs

honey-lemon chicken breasts, 113

horseradish whipped cream, smoked trout fillets with baby greens and, 33–34

hot or sweet Italian sausages, 169

iceberg lettuce, in shredded chicken with peanut sauce, 48–49

in-flight almonds, 57

Italian sausages, hot or sweet, smoked, 169

and peppers, 182–83

in Portuguese-inspired clam and sausage roast, 41

in shrimp and sausage jambalaya, 157–58

jalapeño chiles:

in fresh tomato salsa, 22

in herby chicken breasts with pipérade variation, 115

in mango salsa, 23

in smoked corn and black bean salad, 80–81

in smoky-spicy salsa, 21

jambalaya, shrimp and sausage, 157–58

Jarlsberg cheese:

in baked macaroni and cheese with smoked chicken, 123–24

in smoked chicken, pecan, and Gruyère salad, 74–75

jerky, beef, 42–43

"jigsaw" croutons, 89

juniper berries, in garlic-studded loin of pork, 172–73

kabobs, beef, pepper, and red onion, 206
kidney beans, red, in monster minestrone,
    60–62

lamb:
    chops, smoking of, 196
    leg of, butterflied, with roasted potatoes, Greek
        style, 208–9
    toasted couscous, spring vegetable salad and,
        78–79
leeks:
    cleaning of, 61
    fettuccine with smoked salmon, and peas,
        146–47
    in monster minestrone, 60–62
    in smoked cod with bacon and cabbage, 152–53
    in smoked salmon gone to heaven, 144–45
    in smoked salmon pâté, 39–40
    in smoky mussel chowder, 72–73
lemon:
    -honey chicken breasts, 113
    -tarragon rub, 26
lemonade, 119
lima beans:
    baby, in country style pork and white bean
        casserole, 178–80
    in smoked pork medallions with shameless
        succotash, 181
lime(s):
    juice, in margaritas, 200–201
    in my favorite fajitas, 197–99

macaroni and cheese, baked, with smoked chicken,
    123–24
mackerel, smoked:
    fillet, 136
    in MV fish cakes, 159–60
Madeiras, in smoky chicken liver mousse with
    pumpernickel melba toasts, 44–45
mango salsa, 23
maple mustard glaze, 168

margaritas, 200–201
mayonnaise:
    in deli-style chicken (or turkey) salad, 120
    in green goddess sauce, 17
    in not-your-mother's onion dip, 56
melba toasts, pumpernickel, smoky chicken liver
    mousse with, 44–45
mesclun:
    in smoked chicken, pecan, and Gruyère salad,
        74–75
    in smoked corn and black bean salad, 80–81
    in smoked trout fillets with baby greens and
        horseradish whipped cream, 33–34
Mexican tortilla and smoked corn soup, 66–67
minestrone, monster, 60–62
Monterey Jack cheese:
    in smoked chicken and black bean quesadillas,
        46–47
    in vegetarian chiles rellenos, 231–32
mousse, smoky chicken liver, with pumpernickel
    melba toasts, 44–45
mozzarella, smoked, 53–54
    orzo salad with broccoli, garlic chips and, 87–88
mushroom:
    -barley-turkey soup, 68–69
    triple, beef tenderloin steaks, 204–5
    see also specific mushrooms
mushroom-herb rub, 27
    in herby chicken breasts with pipérade, 114–15
    in triple mushroom beef tenderloin steaks,
        204–5
mussel(s):
    chowder, smoky, 72–73
    smoking of, 141
mustard maple glaze, 168
MV fish cakes, 159–60
my favorite fajitas, 197–99

navy beans, in country style pork and white bean
    casserole, 178–80
not-your-mother's onion dip, 56

salad, warm, crispy-velvet tofu with, 233–34

scrambled eggs with smoked portobellos, and fontina cheese, 226

and smoked shrimp filling, phyllo pastry tartlets with, 50–51

spinach, baby:

smoked chicken, pecan, and Gruyère, 74–75

in smoked trout fillets with baby greens and horseradish whipped cream, 33–34

split pea and smoked turkey soup, 70–71

spread, smoked trout and chive cream cheese, 32

stir-fry, tea-smoked shrimp and asparagus, 150–51

stovetop smokers and smoking:

doneness and, 10–11

frequently asked questions about, 6–9

healthfulness of, 7

large items and, 5

multi-meal preparation and, 11

principle of, 3

safety tips for, 12

seasonings with, 10

sizes of, 3

small or soft-textured items and, 6

sources for, 2

as steamers, 4

using of, 3–5

string bean(s)

in monster minestrone, 60–62

smoked chicken, and cauliflower casserole, 121–22

in turkey-mushroom-barley, 68–69

strip steaks, smoking of, 192

stuffing, quail with wild rice, 130–31

succotash, shameless, smoked pork medallions with, 181

swordfish:

chef Walsh's, with radicchio and papaya salad, 155–56

steaks, smoking of, 137

tarragon:

in fettuccine with smoked salmon, peas, and leeks, 146–47

in green goddess sauce, 17

-lemon rub, 26, 26

tartlets, phyllo pastry, with smoked shrimp and spinach filling, 50–51

tequila, in margaritas, 200–201

teriyaki glaze, quickie, 167–68

thermometers, instant-read, 10

thyme, in bronzed sea scallops with chunky tomato vinaigrette, 148–49

toasted:

couscous, lamb and spring vegetable salad, 78–79

pita chips, 55

tortilla strips, 67

tofu:

crispy-velvet, with warm spinach salad, 233–34

smoking of, 221

tomatillo, smoked sauce, 15

tomato(es):

in country style pork and white bean casserole, 178–80

fresh, salsa, 22

in Mexican tortilla and smoked corn soup, 66–67

in shrimp and sausage jambalaya, 157–58

smoked, sauce, 14

in smoked corn and black bean salad, 80–81

sun-dried, in orzo salad with smoked mozzarella, broccoli and garlic chips, 87–88

in vegetarian chiles rellenos, 231–32

vinaigrette, chunky, in bronzed sea scallops with, 148–49

tomatoes, cherry:
  bow tie pasta with smoked shrimp and, 85–86
  in tuna and white bean salad, 82
tomatoes, plum:
  in fresh tomato salsa, 22
  in rigatoni with smoked turkey and hot cherry
    peppers, 126–27
  in smoked tomato sauce, 14
  smoking of, 212
  in smoky-spicy salsa, 21
tortilla(s)
  corn, Cheddar, and red onion, 222–24
  in my favorite fajitas, 197–99
  in smoked chicken and black bean quesadillas,
    46–47
  and smoked corn soup, Mexican, 66–67
  strips, toasted, 67
triple mushroom beef tenderloin steaks,
    204–5
trout, smoked:
  and chive cream cheese spread, 32
  fillets with baby greens and horseradish whipped
    cream, 33–34
  whole, 138–39
tuna:
  preserved, Sicilian style, 154
  steaks, smoking of, 137
  and white bean salad, 82
turkey:
  -mushroom-barley soup, 68–69
  salad, deli-style, 120
turkey, smoked:
  breast, 103–4
  hash, 125
  rigatoni with hot cherry peppers and, 126–27
  and split pea soup, 70–71
  thighs, 105
  whole, 101–2
  wings, 106–7

ultimate corn bread, 229

vegetable(s):
  spring, toasted couscous and lamb salad, 78–79
  see also specific vegetables
vegetarian chiles rellenos, 231–32
vinaigrette, chunky tomato, bronzed sea scallops
    with, 148–49

walnuts:
  in pesto, 63
  in quail with wild rice stuffing, 130–31
  in smoked chicken, pecan, and Gruyère salad,
    74–75
  in spaghetti with portobellos and parsley pesto,
    227–228
watercress, shredded duck, toasted hazelnut salad,
    76–77
whipped cream, horseradish, smoked trout fillets
    with baby greens and, 33–34
white bean(s):
  and pork casserole, country style, 178–80
  in smoked salmon gone to heaven,
    144–45
  in smoky mussel chowder variation,
    73
  and tuna salad, 82
wild rice stuffing, quail with, 130–31
wine, red:
  in Portuguese-inspired clam and sausage roast,
    41
  in rigatoni with smoked turkey and hot cherry
    peppers, 126–27
  in smoked Italian sausage and peppers,
    182–83
world's best garlic bread, 52

yellow bell peppers:
  beef, and red onion kabobs, 206
  in herby chicken breasts with pipérade,
    114–15

zucchini, in monster minestrone, 60–62